Political Economy

POLITICAL ECONOMY
Politics and Policy Analysis

ROBERT EYESTONE
University of Minnesota

MARKHAM PUBLISHING COMPANY/CHICAGO

MARKHAM POLITICAL SCIENCE SERIES
Aaron Wildavsky, Editor

Axelrod, *Conflict of Interest*
Barber, *Citizen Politics: An Introduction to Political Behavior,* Second Edition
Barber, ed., *Power to the Citizen: Introductory Readings*
Bullock and Rodgers, eds., *Black Political Attitudes: Implications for Political Support*
Cnudde and Neubauer, eds., *Empirical Democratic Theory*
Coplin, *Introduction to International Politics: A Theoretical Overview*
Coplin, ed., *Simulation in the Study of Politics*
Coplin and Kegley, eds., *A Multi-method Introduction to International Politics: Observation, Explanation, and Prescription*
Dolbeare and Dolbeare, *American Ideologies: The Competing Political Beliefs of the 1970s*
Dvorin, ed., *The Senate's War Powers*
Greenstein, *Personality and Politics: Problems of Evidence, Inference, and Conceptualization*
Greenstein and Lerner, eds., *A Source Book for the Study of Personality and Politics*
Lane, *Political Thinking and Consciousness*
Lyden and Miller, eds., *Planning-Programming-Budgeting: A Systems Approach to Management,* Second Edition
McDonald, *Party Systems and Elections in Latin America*
Mitchell, *Public Choice in America: An Introduction to American Government*
Mitchell, *Why Vote?*
Payne, *The American Threat: The Fear of War As an Instrument of Foreign Policy*
Ranney, ed., *Political Science and Public Policy*
Ross, *American National Government: An Introduction to Political Institutions*
Ross, ed., *Public Choice and Public Policy: Seven Cases in American Government*
Ross and Mitchell, eds., *Introductory Readings in American Government*
Russett, ed., *Economic Theories of International Politics*
Sharkansky, *Public Administration: Policy-Making in Government Agencies,* Second Edition
Sharkansky, ed., *Policy Analysis in Political Science*
Strickland, Wade, and Johnston, *A Primer of Political Analysis,* Second Edition

Printed in U.S.A.
Library of Congress Catalog Card Number: 72-163338
Hardcover Standard Book Number: 8410-3030-8
Paperback Standard Book Number: 8410-3052-9

Preface

In *The New Industrial State* (Houghton-Mifflin, 1967), John Kenneth Galbraith asserts that there is an increasing convergence of economic interest between government and technologically oriented business. If his persuasive argument is substantially correct, then it represents a very serious challenge for modern political theory. The prescriptions offered by political theorists are almost universally based on the assumption that the governmental is ultimately separable from the nongovernmental, and that this distinction closely parallels the distinction between public and private forms of activity. With these categories seemingly breaking down, there is more need than ever for some clear, usable concept of the differences between the institutions of business and government.

This book is partly a response to the challenge of Galbraith's thesis. It is not a reform text, however, for that would demand much more attention to political feasibility than I have been able to give in a work of this length. It is instead an analytical text, which proposes a concept of governmental economic intervention and explores the extent of its applicability to some pressing contemporary economic problems.

The distinction of public from private is indeed becoming blurred, as nongovernmental centers of economic power become more concentrated and as governments become increasingly involved in the everyday workings of the economic system. But interaction between government and nongovernmental economic actors does not necessarily mean identity of the two, for each side can bring differing goals to the interaction. I have argued for a view of governments as the legitimate spokesmen for public interests and public purposes, and I have argued for governmental intervention in economic processes to bend them to the service of public purposes. Cooperation between business and government is certainly to be expected, and even encouraged, once a new set of social goals has been selected through the political process.

Neo-Marxists would argue that business is already so completely in control of government that any independent governmental decisions are impossible. For them, business-government interaction has somehow resulted in the subordination of public power to private ends. I do not accept this argument, at least in its extreme form. Indeed, the first half of this book is implicitly a rebuttal to it. By examining in detail the politics of economic policy making I have attempted to assess the present extent of government-business convergence and to show that there are possibilities for independent political action. It may be true that American politics has a business bias, and it certainly is true that special interests have entrenched positions of political power; but it does not follow from these observations that the situation is as hopeless as Marxists assert.

Many of the arguments advanced in this book necessarily rest on examples or on impressionistic evidence. The reader is urged to consider this treatment of the American political economy as only one interpretation, and he should refer to the concluding bibliography for other approaches and other interpretations.

Several people, aside from the author, have attempted to improve this book. My thanks go to William C. Mitchell and Aaron Wildavsky, to my Minnesota colleagues Theodore Marmor and Enid Curtis Bok Schoettle, and to the patient people at Markham. Many rough spots in the text were smoothed out by my wife, Susan, whose commas the careful reader may appreciate. Any errors that have escaped this barrage of advice I happily acknowledge as my own.

Robert Eyestone

Contents

1

What Is Political Economy?

Political Economic Practice in Several Societies

Economics and political science have tended to diverge in the subjects they treat and the methods they bring to bear on their subject matter, while at the same time national policy makers find economics and politics increasingly linked in major policy decisions. Modern Presidents look upon economic prosperity as the cornerstone of successful domestic policy, and they rely on their Council of Economic Advisers for crucial information in a variety of policy areas. Economists find their way into many top administrative positions because their technical knowledge makes them especially valuable as administrators and policy makers. Even Congress, through its Joint Economic Committee, is coming to grips with the economic aspects of the political decisions it makes every session.

This conjunction of economics and politics in the world of public policy decisions calls for a similar conjunction in the theoretical treatment of economic and political questions. Some explicit combination of economic analysis and political analysis is needed for the increasing body of policy decisions in which the economic and political aspects cannot reasonably be separated. It is this reviving body of knowledge, "political economy," that is the subject of this book.

Political economy can be thought of as a body of suggested practices for solving the basic economic problems of a society. Thus the advice of the political economist will differ from one society to another because political goals may differ or because economic problems may take different forms in different societies. Historically, political economy has served a wide variety of purposes. In medieval times political economic thought was largely subordinated to religious thought, both being concerned to guide the individual to his reward in the afterlife. As part of its concern for the individual's salvation, medieval economic thought frowned on the charging of interest on loaned money. Later, during the early colonial period of European history, political economists advised monarchs and princes in the proper course of action to expand their domains. This body of thought, known as mercantilism, advocated low domestic wages, population expansion, and a favorable balance of trade to bring precious metals into the country. In contemporary socialist countries, by contrast, political economic thought seeks to maximize the rate of industrial growth through the internal shifting of resources from consumption goods to education and the production of industrial hardware.

Where can we find the common elements in this disparate collection of purposes to which political economy has been put? Obviously the underlying goals are not similar—what could be more dissimilar than the medieval quest for life after death and the modern capitalist quest for immediate consumer goods? The similarity is found instead in the approach to the solution of economic problems. In each case political economy indicates how basic economic decisions can be made, consistent with the prevailing beliefs of the society in question.

These common economic problems faced by all societies are (1) what is to be produced, (2) by what means it is to be produced, and (3) how the products are to be distributed. In other words, every society must maintain a production system, which mobilizes resources and allocates social effort, and a reward system, which distributes production so as to provide incentives to continued productive effort. In every society, however, these economic goals must be met in a manner consistent with society's beliefs about the appropriate ways to organize production and rewards. "Must" here means simply that if a society is to be reasonably stable and if its citizens are to be content with their lot, then some kind of consistency between the beliefs of the citizenry and the actual operation of the economic system seems to be necessary. In the absence of such agreements there is likely to be either long-run social instability and economic disruption or modification of the economic system toward greater agreement with the beliefs of the citizenry.

In the medieval period, for example, one of the factors in the long term decline of church influence over economic affairs was the growth of opportunities for entrepreneurial and capitalist ventures through foreign trade and the rising city culture.[1] Similarly, many contemporary socialist countries have drawn back from their emphasis on industrial growth and are now also paying some attention to consumer goods, partly because they can now afford to do so, but also partly because their populations are no longer contented with the earlier development priorities.

The Role of Government in Political Economy

How are the dominant beliefs of a society expressed, and how do they affect the operation of economic institutions? Certainly, much of the effect that social beliefs have on economic practices takes place quite unconsciously. If entrepreneurial activity is frowned upon, for example, few people will attempt to become entrepreneurs. If the small independent businessman is highly regarded by a society, then many people will attempt to start their own small businesses. If the heir of an established family is more respected than the man of self-made wealth, then there will be less social incentive for self-made men. And so on.

Increasingly, however, government is becoming an effective instrument of communal beliefs. Governments are granted wide power to rearrange the economic system, either by adjusting production priorities and methods or by altering the distribution of rewards that would otherwise prevail. The impact of governmental actions is easy to see in the three earlier historical periods mentioned above. In the medieval period, the church, through its influence over temporal rulers, was instrumental in maintaining the feudal economic system; encouraging laws against usury; and directing resources to religious art, religious learning, and cathedral building rather than toward empire building or improvement of the economic status of the mass of the population.

In the mercantile period, government encouragement and regulation of business were directed toward national growth and the conquest of foreign markets, even though such policies were not always in the best interests of businessmen. They benefited from mercantilism, but they also chafed against some of the limitations imposed on them by their sovereign in the interests of empire.[2]

In contemporary socialist states it is obvious that the government intervenes in the economic system; indeed, the ultimate goal of socialist economic theory is for all production and distribution decisions to be made by the government acting in the name of the people and for their benefit.

Only in the case of contemporary capitalist systems does it seem strange to attribute a large measure of economic control to the government, although even here large changes have taken place in the last fifty years. Modern economic thought, and hence modern political economy, is largely conditioned by the liberal, individualistic view prevalent in Western philosophy. Roughly speaking, democracy is the political theory fostered by the individualistic world view, and free enterprise is its economic theory. Thus modern political economy grows out of the economics of free individual business enterprise and is associated in its most extreme statements with the doctrine of laissez faire.

In principle, these ideas imply that governments should refrain entirely from any attempt to modify the operation of the economy. Under this view, the market and the price mechanism are the ideal instruments for deciding what shall be produced and who shall be rewarded for productive efforts. Production decisions are made entirely on the basis of demand shown in the market for goods and services, and rewards are distributed according to the usefulness of the talents each individual brings to the market for productive factors. In a philosophical sense, these are ideal solutions to the economic problems of production and distribution; because they are not centrally enforced they allow the individual freedom of choice, and because they are efficient they tend to maximize the total amount of production.

Laissez faire theorists do allow a "caretaker" role for government. Maintenance of the rule of law, for example, obviously must be carried out by some agency for all the people. Common defense is also considered a legitimate concern of the laissez faire government. These exceptions, while they are perhaps important as theoretical precedents for later expansion of government activity, are usually relegated to very unimportant positions by political theorists.[3]

But pure laissez faire has never been an accurate description of the role of government in economic affairs, even in the United States; therefore, a realistic modern doctrine of political economy must deal in positive terms with governmental intervention and governmental responsibility. The wall that would separate government from the economy has been breached in several ways, all of them important for political economy.

Beginning in the early years of American history, a series of political decisions has committed public resources (derived from taxation) to subsidize, regulate, and manage an ever increasing collection of economic activities. These decisions, which are essentially political rather than economic, produce effects on the total economy that are incidental to their main political purpose. But a number of incidental programs, when taken together, may produce a substantial impact, as will be shown in Chapter 2.

Also, governmental responses to a number of real and imagined emergency situations, including depressions and wars, have had lasting impact on the economy beyond that which was thought to be justified by the emergency itself. Thus, tripartite cooperation among the federal government, industry, and labor unions during the New Deal and also during World War II has carried over to some extent into peacetime. In addition, government defense spending during the Cold War has created substantial ties between the government and large industrial firms and has had an important unintended effect on the structure of the economy. No government, even in the American economy, can spend upwards of $50 billion a year for military hardware without producing some reallocation of resources and some redistribution of rewards.[4]

Finally, the federal government is now committed to conscious and continuous intervention in the American economy to maintain maximum levels of employment and economic growth while holding down the level of price inflation. In the aftermath of the 1930s, faced with the threat of another depression following World War II demobilization, Congress passed the Employment Act of 1946 which explicitly gave the President the responsibility to set and carry out policies designed to maintain economic prosperity. Actions under this policy can be thought of as regular and intentional —their primary effect is expected to be general rather than in any single sector of the economy.

This, then, is the context for political economy in the United States. Briefly, it includes the contradictory elements of a history of extensive governmental intervention, both by intentional and incidental means, and a philosophical tradition that values individual enterprise and governmental nonintervention. Between this tradition and the necessities of the moment, a compromise form of intervention has evolved. The basic question in American political economic thought can therefore be phrased as follows: Under what circumstances is governmental intervention in the market desirable either to impose nonmarket conditions on market transactions or to improve the operations of the market?

This book is loosely organized around this fundamental question, although the question itself is so complex and so dependent on value choices that it is impossible to answer it briefly. The first part of this book provides a descriptive background for American political economy. Chapter 2 outlines the development of governmental techniques for influencing the operation of the economy. Chapters 3, 4, and 5 provide a brief description of the political considerations surrounding intentional and incidental economic policy making at the federal level. The second part of the book develops a form of analysis applicable to current political economic issues in the United States. Chapter 6 examines several possible kinds of political-economic synthesis, considering the situations to which they apply and the value preferences they involve. Chapters 7 through 9 relate these forms of political-economic synthesis to several current issues in American political economy, including the perennial problems of inflation and poverty, and the "new" problem of pollution.

Notes

[1] Henri Pirenne, *Medieval Cities* (Princeton, N.J.: Princeton University Press, 1925), especially the chapter on "Municipal Institutions."

[2] *Medieval Cities, passim.*

[3] Adam Smith, *An Inquiry into the Nature and Causes of the Wealth of Nations* (New York: Modern Library edition, 1937), offers a pure view of laissez faire thought. John Stuart Mill, *Principles of Political Economy* (London: J. W. Parker, 1848), outlines the role of laissez faire government.

[4] For a detailed study of the effects of defense spending, see Bruce M. Russett, "Who Pays for Defense?" *American Political Science Review* 63 (June, 1969): 412–26.

2

The Development of American Political Economy

Some Useful Distinctions

At this point it is useful, perhaps indispensable, to introduce some broad categories for describing the development of American political economy. These categories are intended to emphasize a single idea: that economic intervention on the part of the government, even though it uses an almost endless number of devices, serves a few simple political purposes. Further, the history of American political economy is not a history of accidents, but a history of the development of political purposes and the devices invented to carry them out.

The previous chapter touched briefly on the basic economic problems of all societies: (1) what is to be produced, (2) by what means or under what conditions, and (3) for whom? Most societies have not been content to allow these problems to solve themselves, but they have chosen to intervene to a greater or lesser extent by governmental means so as to effect the kind of solution to economic problems the society desires. Governmental intervention, in contrast to "natural" economic devices like competitive markets, takes place in accordance with certain conscious public purposes and generally produces results that differ from those produced by unfettered economic institutions such as markets and "free enterprise" manufacturers.

Intervention may serve three general purposes, corresponding to the three economic problems common to all societies: subsidization, regulation, and management or direction.

Subsidization is intended to affect the choice of the goods and services to produce in a society, generally by making the production of a given item more attractive than it otherwise would be. If some economic activity—the construction of apartment buildings, for example—is made artificially profitable, more resources will be devoted to it than would otherwise have been, either because resources (capital, construction firms, and the like) are drawn from less profitable activities or because a threatened shift out of apartment construction is halted.

Direct subsidization is relatively rare, although it is by no means unimportant. Agricultural price supports are an outstanding example. Farm prices have not generally been supported by direct payment, however, but more commonly by some form of government guarantee. A typical farm subsidy device is a crop loan offered to a farmer with his unharvested crop as collateral. The size of the loan is determined by applying a fixed support price to the expected crop yield. If the actual market price turns out to be higher than the support price, the farmer will sell his crop in the market and repay the loan, pocketing the difference. If the market price is lower than the support price, the farmer is free to default on his loan. In this case the farmer gets the support price for his crop and the government acquires his crop as "surplus."

Air mail has also been used as a subsidy device. In the early days of air travel, the Post Office encouraged the development of commercial aviation by offering favorable rates for transportation of mail by air. By so doing, the Post Office succeeded in developing a number of air routes faster than they would have developed in response to passenger demand alone.

A favorite device for extending a subsidy is the tax exemption or tax write-off. Builders of apartment housing, for example, are provided an indirect subsidy through the device of accelerated depreciation. By claiming higher depreciation expenses each year than they actually must pay, apartment owners may often appear to be suffering losses on their property and may therefore receive favorable tax treatment which they would not otherwise qualify for.

Regulation is intended to affect the conditions or means by which goods and services are produced and made available to the public. Obviously such a definition is very broad, encompassing a wide range of governmental intervention and a correspondingly large number of regulatory techniques. Only a few examples can be provided here.

One common regulatory device is licensing. Through a licensing procedure a governmental unit may be able to impose minimum standards of skill, quality, or reliability in a good or service. Much of the regulatory licensing in the United States is carried out by the fifty state governments, who in turn frequently pass on the administrative problems of licensing to the group being regulated. This practice is especially common with regard to professional licensing—dentists, doctors and engineers, for example. Generally, professional practice in a state is limited to persons with a state license, and the regulatory procedures stipulate that a certain minimum degree of competence be demonstrated before a license is issued. Criminal penalties are usually established to discourage practice without a license.

A prime illustration of regulatory licensing at the federal level is the radio and television licensing activities of the Federal Communications Commission. The FCC was created by the Communications Act of 1934, following a somewhat chaotic period of licensing beginning in 1912. The FCC's primary task is allocation of scarce broadcasting channel spaces among a large number of potential users so as to provide maximum public service, encourage competition and prevent interference among service classes.

Most broadcast licenses require periodic renewal, and the renewal application provides the FCC with an opportunity to scrutinize the broadcaster's activities to determine whether his license should be renewed. Highly profitable radio and television channels are required to justify their program content as being in the public interest, and renewals may occasionally be withheld until the licensee promises to improve the content of his programming.

The FCC's history illustrates a basic, recurring problem in governmental regulation—the lack of any real definition of the public interest, in whose name regulation is supposedly carried out. The profit motivation of broadcasters is presumed to be legitimate, but somehow it is to be harnessed for public benefit. With no clear guideline for this operation the regulatory agency is left very much on its own.

The broad field of food and drug legislation provides a final example of federal regulatory activity. Included here are such diverse activities as U.S. Department of Agriculture meat inspection, certification of new drugs by the Food and Drug Administration, and more recently, truth-in-packaging laws administered by the Federal Trade Commission. Related developments in consumer protection such as product safety laws and truth-in-lending regulation move far beyond the narrow concept of food and drug control, but they are logical outgrowths of the same regulatory purpose. Although "consumerism" is a relatively new phenomenon at the federal level—not until 1962 did a President present a special consumer message to Congress—it promises to bring about a substantial expansion in the already extensive regulatory powers of the federal government.

Management or *direction* is intended most obviously to supplant or supplement private production, but often the purpose behind such governmental activity is to provide goods or services to a segment of the population that would not otherwise have them. Thus governmental management seeks to make up for deficiencies in the normal distribution of economic rewards by going outside the market to provide goods and services directly to consumers. This characteristic distinguishes governmental management from policies designed to subsidize or regulate, since these latter two types generally work through the market instead of supplanting it.

The Tennessee Valley Authority, a well-known example of

federal management, is the model for a whole system of regional public power agencies that have never been built. While providing a plentiful supply of electric power to a large region of the United States, the TVA also serves as an implicit rate standard for private power companies operating in the same region.

Another area in which the federal government has been an active manager is that of home finance. In this area the government, through the Federal National Mortgage Association, the Federal Home Loan Banks, and other agencies, acts as a substitute banker, stabilizing the mortgage market and stimulating the flow of mortgage funds when general money market conditions are adverse to home mortgage loans.

A third example of governmental management is the Social Security system. Here the government acts as a kind of substitute (though compulsory) insurance agent, providing retirement insurance for large categories of the population that might not otherwise be insured. At its inception in the 1930s, Social Security was justified as simply a social insurance device that would pay for itself through premiums collected as payroll deductions and employer taxes, but additions and modifications to the system reveal its true character. Whenever Social Security coverage is expanded, the newly included beneficiaries have not fully paid for their benefits at the time they enter the program. Thus, there is a hidden element of redistribution in Social Security over and above its insurance characteristics. Medicare is the most recent example of this phenomenon. Doctors' fees under Medicare are supposedly covered by a small monthly insurance premium, but this premium does not cover the full cost of the program, and the rest of the expense must be made up from general revenue funds. Whether by accident or by design, therefore, Medicare serves as a means of providing high quality medical care for large numbers of the over-65 population that otherwise might not be able to pay for it.

The preceding pages have given a sampling of the techniques that have proved useful in implementing the three basic governmental purposes in economic intervention. A further distinction is useful here—that of the level at which the effects of a given kind of intervention are expected to show themselves.

Governmental intervention techniques may have their primary effect at the national or system level, on the one hand, or the subsystem or sector level on the other. In some ways this is an artificial distinction, since the economy is an interrelated system and a change in one part will eventually affect every other part. This systemic character aside, however, some kinds of intervention are designed to have primary effect on only one industry while others use modifications in a given industry as a conscious and calculated attempt to bring about across-the-board change in the economic system. Regulation of railroad rates is an example of sector level intervention while regulation of bank lending rates has become an important tool for regulation of the overall rate of economic growth.

Two Political Economy Snapshots

Although the categories just introduced may seem academic rather than useful, these concepts may be helpful in considering the historical development of American political economy. The primary purpose of this chapter is to give such a historical description. A general idea of development can be gained by examining two snapshots of American political economy at widely separated points in time.

EARLY NINETEENTH CENTURY

Political economy in the early 1800s was dominated by the state governments.[1] States chartered manufacturing, banking, mining, and transportation firms, and participated in the construction of various internal improvements such as canals, turnpikes, and railroads. The states encouraged internal improvements in two distinct ways: first, by actually establishing state companies to build such improvements; second, by providing part of the capital for mixed public-private companies setting out to make a profit in the improvements business.

In the early nineteenth century, state governments also engaged in a surprisingly large amount of direct regulatory activity, including extensive licensing and inspection programs. Licensing targets reflected the differences in the economy of the nineteenth century and that of today: in the nineteenth century state regulation through licensing fell especially on peddlers, innkeepers, and retail merchants of various kinds. The perishable commodities of trade generally came under state inspection, and such important frontier staples as lumber and gunpowder were also subject to state control.[2]

Finally, state governments experimented with direct labor and business regulation designed to help the individual laborer or consumer, including setting maximum limits on hours of work and restrictions on price fixing by businesses.

While the state governments were active, the federal government was not quiescent. The basic pattern of federal intervention in the early 1800s served the same purposes that state activity did: facilitation of western settlement and the development of native industries. Toward these ends the federal government pursued several courses of action. It established a national bank to stabilize banking activities in the country and, in part, to provide a supply of relatively easy money to the frontier where it was greatly needed for settlement. It permitted access to public western lands on increasingly easy terms, culminating in the Homestead Act of 1862 by which title could be claimed on the basis of residence alone. Finally it set up a system of tariffs which was basically protectionist in effect, although jockeying for position by various regional interests produced frequent changes in tariff rates throughout the nineteenth century.

Brief mention should also be made of the federal constitutional prohibitions against state currencies, trade barriers, and the like and the provision for a national currency. These actions all went a considerable distance toward nationalizing commerce and opening up trading opportunities across previous colonial boundaries. Both federal and state governments, then, were active in promoting general economic development through encouragement of specific sectors.

IN THE 1970s

Political economy today presents a much different aspect. The economy is highly developed, perhaps even overmature, and governmental policy generally is directed toward managing existing economic activities rather than encouraging new ones. Much state action in the area of internal improvements disappeared after the Civil War, to be replaced by private capital, sometimes aided by foreign sources and sometimes—for the railroads especially—aided by favorable federal policies. In the 1970s only a few areas of federal economic development remain: energy, river and harbor improvements, communications satellites, and the exploration and exploitation of space are the most important examples. While the relative amounts of federal research and development activities are still very large, their economic impact is much more narrow and technical then it was in the nineteenth century.

Many of the regulatory licensing and inspection programs of the state governments have also disappeared; some, like the licensing of local tradesmen, devolved onto city governments, and some, like the inspection of commodities, became largely federalized. Similarly, much labor and business practices legislation has been federalized as well. In addition, the federal government has gone beyond the early state regulatory actions in its detailed regulation of business and manufacturing activities, standards for the packaging and marketing of new products, labor standards, workmen's compensation, and so on.

The national banks had an uncertain career in the 1800s, and they were permanently replaced in 1913 by the Federal Reserve System. In addition, the phenomenal increase in federal taxation and spending, dating in part to the 1930s but more particularly to the cold war period following World War II, has provided a powerful tool for economic regulation through discretionary changes in the tax rate and aggregate spending levels.

The modern tariff, in contrast to pre-1930 tariffs, is generally viewed as an instrument of presidential discretion in foreign policy rather than as a revenue measure or a protectionist device. Protectionist demands have usually been overridden in favor of a lowering of tariff barriers and, in some cases, the complete elimination of tariffs.

Altogether, nationalization of the economy in the 1970s is almost complete. Virtually all manufacturing and wholesale trade takes place in interstate commerce, and federal regulation of interstate commerce generally serves also as regulation of intrastate commerce because of the predominance of the former.

This quick comparison of American political economy snapshots taken 150 years apart shows increasingly effective management at the system level along with more widespread federal involvement in individual sectors. Except for professional licensing, the federal government has almost completely taken over the former state role in economic regulation. In turn, federal regulatory decisions directed toward specific sectors of the economy are now influenced by national (system level) economic goals because they are made in a national political arena. The devices of discretionary monetary and fiscal policy form the cornerstone of the structure of modern political economic policy, and an increasing effort is being made to fit the other, older forms of economic intervention into this structure.

Techniques in the Twentieth Century

The history of system level economic intervention, that is, actions intended to have pervasive nationwide effects, consists of three parallel elements: (1) the emergence of truly national markets for products and productive factors like labor and raw materials, (2) the growing sophistication of our models of the economy and its performance, and (3) the development of techniques themselves, since new techniques open up new possibilities for intervention.

Much of the American frontier was nearly self-sufficient, and any effective attempts to influence the frontier economy must necessarily have been undertaken on the frontier itself. Changes in eastern money markets took a long time to affect the frontier, and their effects were not readily predictable in any case. It was partly for this reason that the major burden of regulatory activity fell upon the states and territorial governments in the nineteenth century. While free land and turnpike construction certainly were conducive to the overall goals of national prosperity and development, each of these individual state actions was also given the more narrow justification of state economic development. By the middle of the twentieth century, however, nearly all the isolated corners of the United States had been brought into a national pattern of trade. The phrase "Prices slightly higher west of the Rockies" marks an economic era that has largely passed. With the growth of western and southern manufacturing since World War II, goods and most types of labor now travel to markets throughout the country.

The development of adequate economic models is partly a technical feat of measurement and partly a question of economic theory. For purposes of economic monitoring it is necessary to specify some measurable economic goals and then to determine how to gather reliable data about these goals, filtering out such confusing factors as normal seasonal trends in economic activity. In the United States most of our economic reporting system was invented "under the gun" in the 1930s in response to congressional and Presidential requests for up-to-date information on employment and production during the depression. There is still room for improvement in our economic indicators: it is commonly accepted that there may be errors of as much as 20 percent in some of our basic economic time series statistics, such as the gross national product. The unemployment rate, however, does somewhat better than this: its accuracy is closer to 5 percent.[3]

But even completely accurate indicators would not be much use without a theory explaining their significance. For such a theory, perhaps the most important step forward is the construction of a dynamic model—one that will predict how far and in what direction a given economic indicator will move if a known change is produced in a variable *that can be controlled by governmental action.* It does a policy maker no good to be able to predict changes in the GNP on the basis of private savings decisions, for example, unless he can also control those savings decisions to some extent. Even an imperfect model relating government spending to changes in the GNP, for instance, could be more useful than a perfect private savings model since governmental spending is more easily manipulated than private saving.

Once such a model exists it can, in principle, be tested and refined until it is suitable as a guide for policy decisions. In practice, though, such a model also requires economic indicators that can anticipate the occurrence of adverse economic conditions. Without such indicators the government would be forced to take emergency action every time it wished to influence the economy because the state of events would never be known soon enough to make moderate policy changes effective.

Somewhat surprisingly, economists even today are not unanimous in their choice of an appropriate economic theory. Until the 1950s the prevailing orthodoxy accepted the work of John Maynard Keynes as definitive. Since the 1950s, however, Keynesian theory, which places major emphasis on governmental taxation and spending decisions, has been criticized by a "Chicago school" of economists who favor greater reliance on monetary devices like the open market operations of the Federal Reserve Board and changes in the Federal Reserve Board's rediscount rate to its member banks. Milton Friedman, the leading spokesman for monetary theory, makes a strong case that such commonly accepted demonstrations of Keynesian doctrine as the 1964 tax cut may be invalid because of the complicating influence of monetary policy changes. The technical arguments of both sides are beyond the grasp of the layman, and apparently there is ground for reasoned differences of opinion even among professional economists.[4]

The final necessary element in system-level economic management, the development of appropriate devices for intervention at that level, may not at first seem to be much of a stumbling block. It is significant, however, because most of the devices useful for system-level intervention were originally invented for purposes other than economic management. The income tax system was created for revenue purposes. (A temporary income tax levied during the 1860s to finance the Civil War was discontinued when it was no longer needed.) Most federal spending programs grew out of the needs of specific sector interests in the economy. The Federal Reserve System originally looked almost wholly to the stability of the banking business for its policy guidelines.

Further, the sum total of federal activity has only recently become great enough to affect the economy by sheer volume. Imagine the plight of President Andrew Jackson in 1835 if he had tried to spur the nation's economy with a budget of less than $50 million, a surplus in the Treasury, and only the tariff for revenue! Since then the powers of the President and other national economic decision makers have been expanded considerably because other forms of governmental economic intervention have come into being and have been found useful in pursuing national economic goals, and also because there have been great increases in the level of federal taxation and spending.

Table 1 outlines the major policy developments in the twentieth century. The time sequence shown in the table is somewhat misleading in that neither the fiscal nor the monetary devices had as much importance at their inception as they have since attained. When the Federal Reserve System was established, for example, discount rate policy was thought to be its most important device,

Table 1
Development of the National Economic Policy Apparatus

Year	*Event*
1913	Beginning of the federal income tax
1913	Creation of the Federal Reserve System
1921	Establishment of a unified federal executive budget
1935	Beginning of national Old Age, Survivors and Disability Insurance (OASDI or Social Security)
1935	Nationalization of unemployment compensation programs
1946	Employment Act of 1946 created Council of Economic Advisers and established the President's responsibility for economic prosperity
1951	The "Accord," under which the Federal Reserve Board gained freedom to pursue policies independent of the needs of the Treasury

and it was not until the mid-1920s that the effectiveness of open market securities purchases was discovered. The greater flexibility of open market operations added considerably to the power of the "Fed," making it the primary national economic tool until the depression of the 1930s.

Fiscal policy was limited in effect prior to the Great Depression for two reasons. Until the 1930s the federal budget was not large enough to be a significant factor in the national economy even if it had been manipulated according to Keynesian strictures. Not until 1931 (disregarding temporarily swollen budgets associated with World War I) did national public sector expenditures reach 5 percent of the GNP. Equally important was the impact of the budgetary philosophy prevalent prior to the New Deal. The central budgetary control given to the President in 1921 was generally employed in the service of economy and a balanced budget. When an economic downturn cut into governmental tax revenues, budget control was used to cut back expenditures to maintain fiscal balance. Conversely, in a booming economy federal spending could expand because the tax system was bringing in more revenue. Thus, federal policy through the Hoover administration exacerbated economic cycles, and it is probably fortunate that the net impact of governmental finances was not very great. State and local governments used similar budgetary techniques, of course, and it is significant that federal spending did not regularly exceed the total of state and local spending until 1940.

Franklin D. Roosevelt campaigned on an "economy" platform in 1932, but he quickly discovered that the depression relief schemes of his advisers required massive and unprecedented deficit spending. It is debatable, though, whether the New Deal of the 1930s constituted a firm precedent for routine and continuous governmental economic intervention. Many of its programs were hastily conceived and were viewed at the time as strictly emergency measures. Mistaking progress for recovery, Roosevelt himself returned to a balanced budget in the late 1930s and brought about a temporary reversal of economic growth in 1938, following several years of deficit-spurred recovery. In any case, the massive

Keynesian prescription for depressions is not directly suited to routine economic management. Continuous management implies more sophisticated techniques and more precise statistics than those available in the New Deal emergency.

A more lasting contribution that can safely be ascribed to the New Deal is the establishment of the most important "automatic stabilizers" in the economy, Social Security benefits and unemployment compensation payments. These two forms of transfer payment act in a manner counter to "budget balancing" since they both result in more net government spending in a slack economy than in a prosperous one.

Continuous peacetime federal responsibility for economic prosperity is generally dated to the Employment Act of 1946. This act gave official status to the national economic goals of full employment, price stability, and economic growth, and, in international relations, a favorable balance of trade. In principle the Employment Act was a sweeping advance over the ad hoc economic policies of the 1930s, although its genesis was short-term concern about a possible postwar recession. Further, although the general terminology of the act was Keynesian, Congress was careful to encourage maximum reliance on private initiative and it did not direct the President to use any specific techniques in carrying out his duties under the act.[5]

Another legacy of World War II was a large public debt. Until 1951 the Federal Reserve Board kept this debt burden in mind when making policy decisions, generally trying to pursue a course of "easy money" to lessen the problems of the Treasury Department in financing and refinancing this debt through government bonds and Treasury notes. But in 1951, under Korean war inflationary pressures, the Fed and the Treasury reached their famous Accord in which the Fed was granted more freedom to make monetary policy as it saw fit, generally meaning tighter money and higher interest rates.

The final steps in this long process of development have taken place in the last decade, with the 1964 tax cut and the 1968 tax surcharge. The 1964 tax cut represents the more significant advance; it is the first peacetime tax cut dictated solely by economic sluggishness. The 1968 surtax is a corresponding response to excess demand in the economy, although part of that demand pressure was generated by unplanned budget deficits resulting from rapid increases in Vietnam war spending in 1965–67.

Further expansion of economic management is still possible, and several proposals have already been advanced that would give Presidents automatic discretionary power over tax rates within a narrow range—up or down 5 percent, for example—but there is no sign that any proposal of this kind will be enacted in the near future.

In principle, Presidents now have an arsenal diverse and powerful enough to carry out their economic management responsibilities. In practice, a President shares control of every policy instrument with other political actors whose perspectives and responsibilities often differ from his own. These differences form one of the bases for the political struggles involved in setting national economic policy. The other major factor contributing to economic policy politics is that the operation of this complex array of high-powered devices is not neutral. While everyone benefits from prosperity and price stability, some benefit more than others because of the nature of the devices used to achieve prosperity. The next three chapters attempt to describe the biases of economic policy politics, first by examining the general value pattern supporting the American economy and then by looking closely at the politics of the various devices used for economic intervention.

Notes

[1] This section draws heavily on Carter Goodrich, ed., *The Government and the Economy: 1783–1861* (Indianapolis: Bobbs-Merrill, 1967).

[2] For a detailed study of state regulation, see Louis Hartz, *Eco-*

nomic Policy and Democratic Thought: Pennsylvania, 1776–1860 (Cambridge, Mass.: Harvard University Press, 1948).

[3] Oskar Morgenstern, *On the Accuracy of Economic Observations* (Princeton, N.J.: Princeton University Press, 2nd rev. ed. 1963); "The Jobless Rate," *Wall Street Journal,* February 6, 1970.

[4] For example, see Milton Friedman and Walter W. Heller, *Monetary vs. Fiscal Policy* (New York: Norton, 1969).

[5] Stephen K. Bailey, *Congress Makes a Law* (New York: Columbia University Press, 1950).

3

A Prelude to Politics

Business Values and the Welfare State

The United States has been described as a business society. It has also been called a welfare state. Both views are partly correct, but their apparent contradiction should alert us to some of the peculiarities of American economic rhetoric. How a welfare state grew up and found secure lodging in a society dominated by business values is a fascinating but lengthy story. More important here is an understanding of the pervasive influence of these divergent traditions on American economic policy.

Like most products of the American political process, the American welfare state is a conglomeration of ad hoc programs created at different times for a variety of purposes. It has been described by one economic historian as "a democratic response to the whole range of popular interests, values and aspirations." [1] Roughly speaking, the concept of a welfare state implies an active government that concerns itself with overall economic prosperity, maintains an elaborate social insurance and economic security program for its citizens, regulates labor-management relations with a labor bias, and redistributes income through progressive taxation and a large government budget.[2]

Except for official concern with prosperity, which is a relatively recent addition, the welfare state as it exists in the United

States implements these principles with a number of gaps and inconsistencies. True, we do have income and health insurance programs, but their coverage is incomplete and often inadequate in level. We do encourage unionism but we also encourage business, and we impose a variety of restrictions on both. Federal income tax rates are progressive in character, but their effects are largely negated by regressive state and local sales and property taxes and by a variety of "loopholes" open to people in the upper income brackets. Thus the American welfare state embodies an imperfect commitment to the welfare of individual Americans. Viner, in a telling phrase, has described it as a "bourgeois welfare state" in contrast to the "proletarian" welfare states of the European countries.[3]

Viner's incongruous notion hints at some of the value assumptions that lie behind American political economy. Obviously a bourgeois society would have a bourgeois welfare state; the strange thing is why it should have a welfare state of any kind. A bourgeois welfare state—one that envisions only minor redistribution of wealth, one not forced to provide for bare subsistence, one existing primarily for social convenience—is sufficient only if nearly everyone in the society is or has the opportunity to become bourgeois. Americans have traditionally believed that this was literally true, and to a large extent they still do believe it. The key to success in this ideal vision of America is the ethic of self-sufficiency, hard work and self advancement. For many nineteenth century settlers, of course, this vision was literally correct. Both frontier society and city society in the rapidly expanding economy offered many routes to moderate wealth for the clever and ambitious.

Naturally, the image of the self-reliant individual does not fit well with a paternalistic state. Paternalism is both unnecessary and undesirable: unnecessary because the individual's welfare is in his own hands, and undesirable because the bountiful state destroys initiative and seduces the individual from his proper course of activity. The more appropriate model for the state in these circumstances is the classic nineteenth century liberal one of laissez faire, in which governments intervene only to defend private property, to provide for common defense, or to supply other basic public necessities. Parallel to the laissez faire state is the free enterprise capitalist economy, where competition is stiff but entry is relatively easy. The economic hero in this picture is the entrepreneur who starts with a small capital investment, takes risks, and applies ingenuity to build a fortune.

The reader may notice that a paradox is built into this picture: one measure of the successful entrepreneur is that he has become large enough or rich enough to escape the risks and uncertainties of the competitive market. A few particularly skillful or lucky entrepreneurs followed just this route in the latter half of the nineteenth century, building large personal empires through expansion and merger. The Rockefeller, Mellon, and Carnegie fortunes, for example, date from this era. Profit was still the basic economic motive for these men, even though the rigors of competition had been left behind, since company profit still translated directly into wealth for the owner of the company.

The rise of industrial monopolies did not in itself change the political views of American business, and governmental policy between the Civil War and the end of the nineteenth century is noteworthy for its extreme favorability to business enterprise. Tariffs were generally set at high levels, for example, and regulative fetters on monopoly were few. During this period, laissez faire and its quasi-scientific social philosophy, social Darwinism, were widely invoked by business and political leaders to justify the business bias in government policy.[4]

Occasions for change in the ideology of American business began to appear in the last quarter of the nineteenth century with the rise in importance of the publicly-owned corporation. In contrast to the family-owned firm and the empire built on trusts and holding companies (the principal forms of economic enterprise in the early period), the publicly-owned corporation gained capital for growth and diversification through public sale of stock shares representing ownership of the corporation's assets. According to the famous thesis of Adolf Berle and Gardiner Means, in *The Modern Corporation and Private Property,* the corporate form separates ownership and management, with the result that management becomes a lucrative and respected profession and profit recedes from its position as the exclusive guide to production decisions.[5] What then supplements the personal profit motive? How does the modern corporation explain itself to the public? What role does it assign to governmental action in the economy?

One response of the mature corporation is the doctrine of "corporate conscience" or "corporate responsibility" in which some corporations claim a concern for society and, it is hoped, commit some of their resources to the solution of social problems.[6] In itself this doctrine is incomplete as a political theory since it does not call for any particular pattern of governmental action. Its import is not very different from that of laissez faire capitalism in that it implies the sufficiency of private initiative to solve society's problems. But the public roles of corporate managers suggest that they now acknowledge the need for supplemental public action. Many of them have taken up dual careers in private and public service, through leadership of governmental study commissions, participation in cooperative programs with government, or temporary government administrative service.

The similarity of management problems in business and government is one obvious reason for heavy cross traffic between the two. Another is the continuous cooperative experience, dating back to World War II, carried out through government research and production contracts. But personal values appear to be operating as well, since many corporate presidents serve government as "dollar-a-year" men in addition to their regular occupation, and some take substantial pay cuts to go into public service.

Whatever the reasons, there is no doubt that the ideology of large corporations has changed from that of either the "robber barons" or of the struggling individual entrepreneur. It includes a greater tolerance and even encouragement of positive governmental activity, but the principles for deciding when public action is necessary and the formulas for appropriate limits on government are now even less clear than they were in the nineteenth century. John Kenneth Galbraith in *The New Industrial State* has tried to present a plausible corporate political philosophy based on the planning needs of large technological firms,[7] but his argument is not widely accepted by economists as a correct description of the American economy, and in any case it would apply in a strict sense to a relatively small proportion of all producers.

It is probably futile to attempt to determine what American business "demands" of government, since concerted business pressure is a rare occurrence. More often American business acts in a defensive manner, seeking to maintain customary practices and protect vested interests and established privileges. While free enterprise rhetoric may be invoked in this political struggle, the piecemeal nature of the combat creates no positive rules for governmental action. In operation, then, the ideology of American big business is quite pragmatic: it defends in some areas and permits in others, but it rarely demands. Arguments ostensibly based on principle are in fact settled by compromise in most cases. Over the last hundred years, this pragmatism has accommodated a substantial increase in regulation and a decline in direct subsidization.

American big business success in weathering changes brought about by the maturing American economy has not propagated the public service ideology to American small business, retailing or the service occupations. Here the notions of laissez faire, free enterprise, and economic competition are expressed in almost pure form. It is only appropriate that they would be so expressed: the model of risky enterprise in a highly competitive market is still a close approximation to the truth for these businesses. Here, also, the social values of individualism, hard work, and thrift find continuing expression as the best way to achieve economic success.

Thus there is considerable variety in the political economic doctrine of American business. The economic circumstances of individual businessmen relate in a rough manner to whether they are willing or unwilling to grant substantial powers of interference to the government. At the same time, many of the segments of the business community most strongly opposed to governmental intervention are the most consistent advocates of governmental devices to "encourage" free enterprise, such as favorable tax treatment for extractive industries and protectionist tariffs for industries faced with foreign competition. Common to all segments of American business—although more often expressed by small business and its spokesmen the U.S. Chamber of Commerce (a private association) and the Small Business Administration (a governmental agency)—is the so-called "Protestant ethic" with its work orientation and emphasis on self reliance.[8]

Business Values in Politics

The vagueness of American business ideology is paralleled by the obscure character of its political impact. One reason for difficulty in linking ideology to specific policies is that the links are pervasive but largely indirect. Business values are propagated by an almost endless variety of means: in advertising, especially the "institutional," image-building variety, which is not directly connected with product sales; in literature of the Horatio Alger sort; through overtime and take-home work pressures within business; through competitive consumption pressures in suburbia; and by countless other means. If these widely shared values have any effect on economic policy it must be an indirect and perhaps unconscious one, operating through vague limits perceived by Presidents and congressmen. Inevitably, such perceptions will be fuzzy, incompletely formed, and possibly contradictory. Nationalization of basic industries is socialistic and therefore un-American, but the Atomic Energy Commission is not. The Tennessee Valley Authority may be socialistic, but Medicare is not (although the American Medical Association said it was). What of the negative income tax, or wage and price controls? These questions are yet to be decided, as are many others. Any a priori formulation of the uniquely "American" answer to these questions is risky and uncertain at best.

Business values may also bear directly on economic policy decisions through direct representations that business firms make to Congress or to the federal executive branch. Both small and large business firms are involved in this process of influence attempts, but their targets and the identity of their most sympathetic governmental listeners are different.

The "public service" corporate executive has been recruited almost exclusively from big business in recent years. Previous contractual relations (especially military), professional associations, and similar personal backgrounds and values all make the higher levels of the executive bureaucracy much more congenial to the big businessman than any other branch of government would be. Two examples are Ben Heineman, a railroad executive who chaired a study commission on a guaranteed income, and David Packard (of Hewlett Packard, the electronics firm), who is an Assistant Secretary of Defense in the Nixon administration.

If these big businessmen are projecting any business values into their relationship with the federal government, it is the general notion of corporate responsibility. By participating in the solution of social problems, they hope to show that big business is not misusing its vast economic power and that a partnership between government and the private sector is possible. The business members of the National Alliance of Businessmen and the Urban Coalition are demonstrating similar concern by participating in quasi-governmental activities aimed at the solution of social problems through voluntary business action.

Small businessmen, by contrast, find the Congress much more congenial than the higher federal bureaucracy, and again personal values and backgrounds are probably important explanations. Many congressmen are still hometown boys, while the executive branch is composed primarily of people with national career patterns. The experience shared by many congressmen, of having been young local lawyers, brings them into extensive contact with local small businessmen either in a legal capacity or socially through businessmen's service clubs such as the Rotary, and these common experiences unquestionably contribute to a common outlook. The impact of small business backgrounds on Congress reinforces the values of self-reliance and independence from governmental control, while at the same time making congressmen more receptive to programs of subsidization directed toward small business. Thus Congress, of all the branches of the federal government, is the stronghold of American small business influence, and small business values inevitably make their mark on nearly every piece of economic legislation passed by Congress.[9]

Direct business pressure group activity is part of the traditional subject matter of political science, but the terms that political scientists customarily use to describe these relationships differ from those in the foregoing discussion. Political scientists pride themselves on their hardheaded realism—they prefer to speak of "pressures" and "interests" rather than "communications" and "values." One point that should be noted here is that this difference in terminology also implies a difference in the concepts themselves. Specifically, it suggests that businessmen may pursue personal interests quite inconsistent with the values that they express publicly. They may, for example, stress the values of free enterprise while simultaneously seeking government subsidies for themselves.

This point leads to a more systematic approach to the politics of economic policy; an approach that outlines the interplay of private economic interests and the broad public purposes that form the ostensible bases for economic policy choices. Every kind of economic intervention, whether specifically business related or not, displays these two aspects. Even regulatory and subsidy programs, directed toward narrowly defined problems in a given sector of the economy, have their public faces. Such programs, when they are discussed in the public forum, are commonly justified in terms of broadly shared public economic goals such as national prosperity or maintenance of the free enterprise system.

The beginnings of modern agricultural policy provide a good example of this duality in economic policy. When price supports were first introduced on a permanent basis in the 1930s they were of course defended as redressing the balance of justice in favor of the farmer, but they were also justified as national policy because national prosperity was alleged to rest on the prosperity of agriculture.

Even college professors, who like to imagine themselves above these things, react in a similar fashion to the availability of federal research funds. Federally sponsored research is justified by its contribution to national security and economic growth, but such programs, simply because they confer privileges and establish vested interests for a clientele group of beneficiaries, create interest groups that attempt to maintain and expand the programs that benefit them. Universities themselves are involved in lobbying for research subsidies, and so also are many of the professional associations to which academic scientists belong.

A complete picture of sector level economic policies, then, has three elements: (1) the immediate sector-level purpose, (2) the private economic interests that gain immediate benefit from the program in question, and (3) the system-level purpose that is used to justify the program to the public at large.

This formula provides a useful perspective for sector-level policies since it makes a distinction, in principle, between real subsidies and quasi-subsidies and between real regulation and quasi-regulatory activity. Tax allowances for depreciation provide an example in the area of subsidization. During 1969, when Congress was examining the 27.5 percent oil depletion allowance as part of general tax reform, the oil companies ran full-page ads in major newspapers attempting to prove that ultimately the public benefited from this tax loophole through lower gasoline prices, better quality, and so on. If this argument is correct, then the oil depletion allowance is only a quasi-subsidy. In fact it would be a case of a "public good," where the public interest would not be adequately served if private oil producers decided how much to spend for research solely on the basis of market considerations. If the argument is false the oil depletion allowance is a true subsidy, and the oil interests have convinced Congress that they are worthy of support regardless of any possible public justification for such support.

In regulatory policies, licensing procedures provide a good test case. We can speak of regulation in the public interest and regulation in the private interest, depending on whether there is an honest public purpose being served by a given licensing procedure. The typical pattern of state professional licensing is one of private interest regulation because the primary effect of the licensing procedure is to allow professions to restrict entry. This kind of guild system can be justified as regulation in the public interest, however, if the general public does in fact derive more benefit from restriction of entry than from the greater supply of services and lower standards that might otherwise result.

The point of these examples is not whether there is a private interest involved, since there always is such a private interest, but whether there is also a public interest being served. It should not be surprising that the extent of public interest is often debatable. The standard of comparison for such arguments is often nonexistent—as in the state regulation case above—or the comparison requires a calculation of future costs and benefits which cannot be made with certainty—as in the oil depletion example. Research and development grants also exemplify a mix of private and public purposes. They subsidize universities and university professors, but they also contribute legitimately to national economic growth.

In any case, these issues need not be resolved here. It is sufficient simply to identify the various patterns that may occur and to seek explanations for their occurrence. Three typical patterns can be identified:

A. System-level effects are not considered in making sector level policies.
B. System-level policy decisions incorporate, and are made consistent with, sector level interests so that both sets of interests are served.
C. System-level policy decisions are made in complete isolation from the political forces surrounding sector level interests.

Each of these patterns appears in economic policy in the United States, as the next chapter will show.

Notes

[1] Jacob Viner, "The United States as a Welfare State," in E. O. Edwards, ed., *The Nation's Economic Objectives* (Chicago: University of Chicago Press, 1964), p. 157.

[2] "The United States as a Welfare State," p .155.

[3] "The United States as a Welfare State," p. 157.

[4] For a more detailed discussion of the laissez faire question in the nineteenth century, see Sidney Fine, *Laissez Faire and the General-Welfare State* (Ann Arbor: University of Michigan Press, 1956).

[5] This thesis is updated in Adolf A. Berle, Jr., *Power Without Property* (New York: Harcourt, Brace & World, 1959).

[6] This general notion is examined critically in Michael D. Reagan, *The Managed Economy* (New York: Oxford University Press, 1963).

[7] John Kenneth Galbraith, *The New Industrial State* (Boston: Houghton Mifflin, 1967).

[8] See John H. Bunzel, *The American Small Businessman* (New York: Knopf, 1962).

[9] Robert M. Heilbroner, interview in *The New York Times,* November 24, 1968.

4

The Political Dynamics of Economic Policies: Subsidization and Regulation

Subsidization

Subsidization policies hope to increase either the quantity of a good or service produced or the amount of a commodity consumed. Subsidies may take the form of direct price support in the market or profit guarantees or guarantees against losses in risky situations. Price support devices are likely to increase production rather than consumption, since they generally raise the market price of the good in question. Guarantees of profit or guarantees against risk are more useful where an increase in consumption is desired, since they do not necessarily raise prices and may allow them to be lowered. These relatively simple devices have proliferated almost endlessly: one study found 1,315 subsidy and quasi-subsidy programs in existence in the 1960s.[1]

Subsidy policies typically follow pattern A in the previous chapter. A new program may start with public support and a broad public justification, but it quickly passes into the hands of an administering bureaucracy and disappears from public view. Subsequent policy revisions are decentralized, being heavily influenced by the bureau or agency in question, the committee or subcommittee of Congress that oversees it, and by the subsidized industry itself. Programs, even though they have justifications in principle, are largely ad hoc responses to political claims and counterclaims. Since there is in fact no overarching subsidy guideline and since policy making is decentralized, claims and counterclaims are often handled by the simple device of inclusion. Each new subsidy involves only a few people and therefore seems to be relatively costless. Subsidies are rarely discontinued because they become intertwined with the organizational goals of their administering agencies and with the careers and advancement prospects of their administrators, and because congressional oversight committees are generally peopled with friendly congressmen.

Overall subsidy policy is not usually consistent because the overall policy is merely an aggregate of a number of separate and unrelated decisions. No supervisory agency has overall policy consistency as its organizational goal, and the complexity of detail makes Presidential control a frustrating task. Then too, individual subsidies are not the stuff of Presidential politics. They are usually too technical and affect too few people to merit much Presidential attention.

Agriculture price supports provide a good example of many of these features of subsidization. Since they were begun in the late 1920s, price supports have been extended to a widening range of crops, long since outrunning the notion of "basic commodities" with which the price support program began (see Figure 1). The only instance of retrenchment for mandatory supports occurred shortly after the end of World War II, when a number of critical war effort commodities were withdrawn from the mandatory list. They remained available to be supported at the option of the Secretary of Agriculture along with almost every major farm commodity in recent years.

The expansion of price support activity has been paralleled by several other developments within agriculture politics. Between

Figure 1
The History of Mandatory Agriculture Price Supports

1938	*World War II*	*1947*	*1949*	*1956*
Wheat Cotton Corn	(Continued) →			
	Tobacco Rice Peanuts	(Continued) →		
	Milk Butterfat Potatoes	(Continued) →		
	Hogs Eggs Chickens Turkeys Dry peas Dry edible beans Soybeans Flax seed (oil) Peanuts (oil) Sweet potatoes Am. Eg. cotton	(Discontinued)		
		Wool	(Continued) →	
			Mohair Honey Tung nuts	(Continued)
				Oats Rye Barley Grain sorghums

the 1930s and the 1960s, agriculture policy became increasingly decentralized in several respects.[2] Programs became increasingly commodity specific. In the 1930s agriculture bills were simple, representing a single program applied to all basic commodities. In the 1940s and 1950s they became omnibus bills encompassing a variety of commodity-specific programs within a single piece of legislation. Finally, In the 1960s the programs for separate commodities were often written and passed as separate bills. Under President Kennedy, Secretary of Agriculture Orville Freeman proposed a scheme that would have gone even farther. In this plan, producer groups for the separate commodities would have drafted their own supply management programs which would then be ratified by the U.S. Department of Agriculture. Congress did not accept this scheme, however, presumably because it bypassed that body as a focus for agriculture policy making.

Throughout this period the congressional agriculture committees themselves became more decentralized. In the 1960s, for example, there was a subcommittee exclusively concerned with feed grains, and another subcommittee for cotton and peanuts. The feed grains group was dominated by midwestern congressmen, where feed grains are important cash crops, while the cotton and peanuts subcommittee was (naturally) composed of congressmen from the southern states.[3]

The history of subsidization of the cotton industry provides another example of an inherent problem with subsidies: their tendency to proliferate. Subsidization of domestic cotton prices improved the economic position of cotton growers, but it weakened the international market position of American cotton exporters. Thus, exporters were granted a subsidy to counter the unexpected side effects of the first subsidy. But both these actions raised the costs of domestic cotton users, and a third subsidy program was passed in the 1960s to aid domestic cotton mills.[4]

One can generally conclude that subsidies always have undesirable side effects, and only an examination of the specific case can reveal whether the side effects are worse than the intended benefits. As a final example, consider the U.S. experiences in subsidizing its shipping industry. One technique used to encourage American shippers is the requirement that American coastal transportation must use American ships. Other than providing an incentive to use other forms of transportation if they are suitable, this device has worked reasonably well. One of its side effects, however, has been substantial harm to the American timber industry. The ship-American requirement has raised domestic timber costs to the point where foreign timber is competitive in many American markets. In the early 1960s American timber concerns were granted emergency exemption from the ship-American rule, but shippers soon became concerned that their subsidy was being undercut. Obviously, there is no easy solution to a conflict of this kind.[5]

Regulation

Regulatory policies are intended to affect the conditions or means by which a given economic activity occurs. Sometimes the motivation for federal regulation has been simply the desire of an industry to impose a single authoritative set of procedures on itself through the mechanism of governmental force. More often, however, regulation has been used to curb private irresponsibility in the public interest—that is, to impose noneconomic conditions on producers in addition to those imposed by the market. Pure food and drug legislation provides an obvious illustration. Antitrust laws—an extreme example of the same general procedure—attempt to substitute for competition in situations where normal market forces have become largely irrelevant to producer decisions.

In nearly every case of public interest regulation, regulatory actions proceed directly from conscious governmental policy decisions. These decisions, in turn, are more or less direct responses to public pressure, public scandal or a presidential initiative taken in the public's name. (The fact that Presidents often have their own political futures in mind when they take such action does not make this statement any less true.) Federal railroad rate regulation and the Interstate Commerce Commission are early examples of such regulatory action; consumer protection legislation is a recent example.

Following the initial passage of regulatory legislation, however, it often follows a course of development similar to that of subsidization.[6] An administrative bureaucracy must be established, either in an existing department or in an independent commission. Bureaucrats often take on the perspective of the industry they regulate, for a number of reasons. Public interest in a given regulatory program generally cannot be sustained for long after the agency has been established. When public attention diminishes, so also does the urgency for close presidential support and supervision. In this situation, bureaucrats—especially those in the independent regulatory agencies—must reach out to their clientele for political support since they cannot expect to get routine support from their department head or from the President. Cooperation is natural and inevitable in any case because the regulated industry has knowledge and expertise necessary for effective regulation, because agencies are expected to consult with their clientele in formulating regulatory rules, and because administrators often come from a background similar to that of the industry leaders.

A commonly observed pattern in regulatory politics is that of the "subgovernment"—a triad formed of industry, agency, and congressional subcommittee.[7] This group acquires de facto responsibility for essentially all policy decisions made with regard to the industry in question. A close working relationship exists among the members of the triad, with the regulatory agency often serving as unofficial governmental spokesman for the interests of the industry. Each of the three partners has little incentive to go outside the triad, hence policy implementation decisions are largely insulated from public view and from public criticism. Most of the old federal regulatory agencies have been described in these terms at one time or another, with the ICC, FCC, and FTC being perhaps the most notable examples.

The career of the Securities and Exchange Commission is an important exception, since it is a regulatory agency that has maintained—or regained—its regulatory vitality. The SEC's success reveals one of the conditions apparently necessary for effective regulation. This agency has relied on voluntary compliance rather than riding roughshod over industry opposition, but it has been successful in gaining voluntary compliance because the securities industry has consciously tried to be self-regulating and because the industry realizes that it is often vulnerable to more stringent controls. In the last few years Wall Street dealers have been unable to cope with the volume of transactions caused by bull market speculation, the growth of mutual funds and the activities of institutional investors, and they have not been able to curb the temptations of some dealers to trade on "inside" information about corporate decisions. Taking advantage of these industry weaknesses, the SEC has taken a hard regulatory line to obtain voluntary industry compliance. If the securities industry had not appeared so vulnerable, it is doubtful that the SEC could have successfully imposed many of the procedural reforms that it did.

Aside from its inherent political difficulties, economic regulation is complicated by the separation of powers and by federalism. Since matter of economic regulation. Previously, however, it staked out World War II, the Supreme Court has deferred to Congress in the an important role for itself in economic regulatory policy, generally applying a strict constitutional interpretation to federal economic powers. Often the courts must work with vague or sweeping congressional policy statements, and in interpreting these statements the judges bring their own standards to bear on cases that come before them. The Sherman Act of 1890, for example, was interpreted in the courts as a less sweeping condemnation of trusts than Congress intended. Among other things, it was held to apply only to attempts to form combinations in restraint of trade, and not to existing monopolies. The Clayton Act of 1914, on the other hand, was held applicable to labor unions by the courts even though unions had been specifically exempted by Congress.

The early days of radio broadcast licensing provide another example. When one of the early channel allocation schemes was invalidated by the federal courts in the 1920s, on grounds that the executive branch did not have power to restrict licensees, the broadcasters themselves in desperation drafted a plan and persuaded Congress to pass it as a substitute. Congress reacted favorably, creating the Radio Act of 1927.

Certainly the most famous case of judicial involvement in economic policy making is the Supreme Court's 1935 decision declaring the National Recovery Administration unconstitutional. NRA, the keystone measure of Roosevelt's depression recovery program, had set up elaborate regulatory structures that almost completely supplanted the market in determining wage and price levels. But this case, while famous, may not have much policy significance because the likelihood of NRA success is a matter of conjecture. It had been in effect scarcely two years and was beginning to encounter business criticism when the Supreme Court struck it down.

In addition to the complications formerly introduced by the separation of powers, federalism continues to add an element of confusion to present regulatory efforts. The essence of federalism is sharing of powers among the several levels of government—national and state in particular. Among the fifty states, however, "competition" is a more appropriate term than "sharing." In the last quarter of the nineteenth century and the first quarter of the twentieth century, for example, a number of states competed among themselves for business incorporations. New York, New Jersey, and Delaware especially offered corporations relative freedom from inspection in exchange for incorporation fees and corporate taxes. This competition substantially undercut the significance of incorporation as a possible regulatory device. It also saddled the federal government with the resulting regulatory problems since it demonstrated the states' disinclination to regulate business incorporations.

In some areas of economic regulation state activities support the old argument that states are experimental "laboratories" within the federal system; in other areas the states have lagged behind the federal government in the expansion of regulatory policies. In the latter case, a federal initiative often preempts the field, so that many states never do establish their own programs once the federal government has acted. Table 2 provides just one illustration of federalism in economic policy—labor legislation. In this area the states sometimes precede the federal government and sometimes lag behind it.

The data in Table 2 are interesting in themselves, but they also hint at a host of regulatory policy problems caused by federalism. Especially in the period when some states have attempted to take regulatory initiative in certain areas, the way is open for numerous legal jurisdictional conflicts. Opponents of regulation will appeal to the federal government against the states, while supporters of regulation will naturally side with the states in their efforts to expand state regulatory power. In these battles the courts

Table 2
History of Selected Federal and State Labor Legislation

Area	*Progression of Legislation*	*Year*
Child labor	First state law (hours)	1842
	First state law (age)	1848
	First federal law	1916
	41 states had an age limit and 17 states had an hours law	1913
Minimum wages	First state law	1912
	First federal law (part of NIRA)	1933
	18 states had minimum wage laws	1933
Workmen's Compensation	First federal law	1908
	First state law	1911
	Half of the states had workmen's compensation laws	1915
Fair employment practices	First federal law (by executive order)	1941
	First state law	1945
	Half of the states had fair employment laws	1965

Source: U.S. Department of Labor, *Growth of Labor Law in the United States* (Washington, D.C.: U.S. Government Printing Office, 1967).

are caught in the middle, attempting to interpret ambiguous constitutional guidelines and vague congressional intentions. In this way many regulatory policy issues are resolved as questions of the federal division of powers even though their real substance revolves around support or opposition to regulation itself.

In one recent example the Minnesota Pollution Control Agency came into conflict with the Federal Atomic Energy Commission over a proposed atomic power plant at Monticello, Minnesota, to be constructed by Northern States Power Company, a private multistate electric utility. Normally the Minnesota PCA grants waste discharge licenses and sets pollution standards for utility service in the state while the AEC regulates domestic uses of atomic energy. Conflict arose when the PCA wished to apply a maximum limit to radioactive discharges from the proposed plant which was only 1 percent of the AEC's standard. The plant became a local *cause célèbre,* and conservation groups picketed the public hearings on its licensing. Minnesota's Governor Harold LeVander was reluctantly drawn into the fray on the side of the PCA, and NSP sided with the Atomic Energy Commission since its plant would meet the AEC's standard but not the standard claimed by the PCA. Utilities in other states naturally watched with great interest to see what precedents would be set by this case.

Monetary Policy as a Form of Regulation

One important special case of economic regulatory activity is the body of techniques commonly called monetary policy. Discretionary monetary policy is, with few exceptions, an instrument controlled exclusively by the Board of Governors of the Federal Reserve System. Its immediate purpose is to regulate the rate at which money can be lent and borrowed, but the indirect intent of such regulation is to stimulate or restrain private economic activity in such a way that stable national economic growth takes place. The Federal Reserve Board is effective for several reasons. It can set the rate at which it will lend funds to its member banks (discount rate changes), which in turn affects the rate at which banks loan money for home mortgages, business expansions, and the like. It can specify how much of its total deposits a bank must maintain as cash in its vaults (changes in the reserve ratio), which in effect adds to or removes from the stock of money in circulation. Finally, it can buy and sell Treasury bills (open market operations); this action also changes the effective stock of money in circulation and therefore the ease or difficulty of financing business expansion.

Of these three devices, the most flexible and most useful are discount rate changes and open market operations. These both work through the market, and depend for their effect on the oligopoly power granted to the Fed by its 5,900 member banks. Reserve ratio changes today are generally thought to be too drastic and too inflexible a device for precise economic regulation. Of the three devices the reserve ratio is the only one that does not operate through the market. It is a straightforward regulatory technique that takes effect prior to any consideration of the money market, and therefore requires the market to adjust to it.

One apparent reason discretionary monetary policy does work is simply that it operates through the market, and therefore voluntarily. It is a nearly perfect example of a system level policy decision dictating the means to be used in a given sector to achieve national economic goals (essentially pattern C described in Chapter 3). The Fed's Board of Governors meets every month to assess the state of the economy and choose appropriate monetary measures. The Fed's actions (aside from reserve ratio changes) do not legally constrain any member bank. They work because member banks respond to the Fed's effect on the money market and because the Fed exercises a kind of moral suasion over the banking community. Bankers generally accept its assessment of the state of the economy as authoritative and are therefore willing to go along voluntarily with the drift of the Fed's actions.

To complete this picture of the Federal Reserve Board's success it need only be noted that its policy decisions are not applied case by case, that they are not subject to judicial review, and that there is little political advantage to be gained by interfering in the Fed's decisions. All three of these characteristics are in marked contrast to most regulatory policies, and the differences account for much of the unusual character of monetary regulation.

The only exception to this picture of monetary policy "nonpolitics" is the banking committees in Congress. These committees have little formal control over the Fed but they can exert political pressure on the banking industry if their chairmen choose to do so. In recent years Representative Wright Patman (D., Texas), Chairman of the House Banking Committee, has been an outspoken critic of tight money. In 1969, for example, he chided the Fed for the adverse effects of its tight money policy on housing construction and he threatened to conduct an investigation into possible collusion when the country's major banks decided to raise their prime lending rates independent of any discount rate change by the Fed. The effect of such actions is hard to assess, but it is possible that banks, and the Fed, are more cautious about money supply constriction with a foe of tight money firmly in command of congressional banking policy.

Subsidy and Regulation: To What Effect?

The enormous variety of federal subsidy programs makes any summary of their effects a difficult task. Since subsidies have been used throughout American history, however, one useful way to summarize their effects is to view them as techniques for implementing national economic development. If this is done it appears that subsidies, taken in the aggregate, have had mixed effects for at least the past 50 years. In the early history of the United States subsidies generally encouraged economic changes already occurring, most notably those associated with settlement and industrialization. In the twentieth century, however, subsidies have both advanced and retarded economic change. Research and development through government contracts have speeded technological developments in electronics, aerospace, and other fields. On the other hand, subsidies extended to the extractive industries, agriculture, and small business have resisted economic changes that would otherwise have taken place. Without subsidies many more family farms would have gone under and the shift toward chain and franchise merchandising would have proceeded much farther than it has.

Table 3 provides a rough picture of the relative dollar impact of the various "subsidy" programs in the federal budget. These figures, generally supporting the conclusions above, should be supplemented in two respects. Military and space spending in the budget contain sizable amounts of research and development expenditure which is of general benefit to society. It is difficult to gauge the dollar value of these benefits, but they must be counted as substantial subsidies. Of course, these are subsidies in which there may be a substantial public interest in addition to the private interests of the subsidized industries since to some extent they upgrade general manpower skills and produce useful technical advances.

Table 3
Budget Expenditures for Selected Functions, 1946–70
(in millions of dollars)

	1946	*1950*	*1954*	*1958*	*1962*	*1966*	*1970*
Agriculture and agricultural resources	743	2,783	2,573	4,419	4,131	3,679	5,181
Space research and technology	—	—	90	89	1,257	5,933	3,947
Commerce and transportation	773	1,863	1,219	1,631	5,410*	7,135	8,969
Community development and housing	−199	262	−628	30	589	2,644	2,772
Health, education, and welfare	1,047	1,985	2,448	3,600	24,077*	35,816	62,853

Source: Budget of the United States Government, 1955, 1963, and 1970 (Washington, D.C.: U.S. Government Printing Office).

* Indicates a change of definition for the statistical series in question.

Second, a number of regulatory policies, essentially costless in terms of budgeted federal expenditures, have substantial subsidy effects. State and federal fair trade and resale price maintenance laws are examples of this kind of "regulatory subsidy." They act as a kind of profit guarantee for small businesses since they make it more difficult for chain stores and discount houses to undercut the prices that small retailers charge for similar items.

Whether subsidies such as these are in the public interest is a question that cannot readily be answered by economics, but may instead be more appropriately treated as a political question of competing values. Fair trade laws can be defended on noneconomic grounds, for example, by their contribution to maintenance of the small independent businessman and to preservation of a personalized, close-to-the-people kind of retailing. The fact that subsidies must be used to pursue these values indicates that the values themselves are in conflict with the economics of the situation, and it also suggests that the impact of subsidies must be judged on several dimensions. It must suffice here to say simply that the noneconomic impact of subsidies has been, on the whole, to encourage and sustain the "traditional" values associated with American small business: individuality, self-reliance, hard work, and independence from governmental control.

The vast panoply of federal economic regulation is not as significant as it may appear on the surface, if by "significant" one means intervention contrary to the interests of private economic actors. Much economic regulation simply regularizes procedures in a given industry, thereby relieving producers in the industry of some of the risks and uncertainties of normal competition. Much of the remaining regulation can be rendered harmless by the processes of regulatory politics described earlier. Occasionally, however, the most moribund of agencies may come to life under the impetus of a dynamic new commissioner, the favor of Presidential attention or the prodding of outside muckrakers.

The Federal Communications Commission is an example of the first situation. When John F. Kennedy became President in 1961 he appointed Newton Minow to the FCC, and Minow promptly embarked on a crusade against the "intellectual wasteland" of television. The Federal Trade Commisison exemplifies the last situation. Long a placid agency, the FTC was stung in 1969 by sharp criticism from Ralph Nader and "Nader's Raiders," enthusiastic young law students who investigated the FTC's procedures and found them wanting in a number of particulars. Later in 1969 the FTC became a more active advocate of consumer protection legislation, as if in reaction to the earlier criticisms brought against it.

The Federal Reserve System, considered a regulatory agency, produces effects that are both beneficial and detrimental to its presumed client, the American banking industry. The range of detrimental effects the Fed's actions can have on banks is limited by the nature of monetary policy (banks can make a profit whether the interest rate is high or low), but the Fed may go against the short term interests of member banks by trying to tighten the money supply when credit is easy, or vice versa. On the other hand, the Fed often supports its member banks in policy conflicts outside the monetary arena. In 1969 the Congress held hearings on bills to limit the issuance of unsolicited bank credit cards. The FTC favored such legislation because it felt banks acted irresponsibly in sending unsolicited credit cards to people who might not normally merit the credit offered to them. The Federal Reserve Board supported its member banks, asserting that the proposed legislation would be an unwarranted interference with bank credit decisions.

Setting aside such specific exceptions, we can conclude that economic regulation definitely runs counter to the preferences of American business to the extent that it is effective. Since most regulatory intervention is intended to serve public (consumer) interests rather than business (producer) interests, it is directly contradictory to the principle of laissez faire, which allows only business protection.

On the surface, regulatory activity that simply maintains regular relations in an industry seems to offer a counter-example to these conclusions. But while such regulation serves private interests, at the same time it probably also serves public interests. It is doubtful whether the public would benefit from chaotic and uncertain conditions in any of the basic U.S. industries—natural gas, for example. Consider an industry like natural gas, in which a large capital investment is required before anything can be produced and sold. In such an industry, cutthroat competition might simply be wasteful of the consumer's money. A form of benign regulation is in everyone's interest in such cases, and perhaps it is this kind of economic regulation that is the most significant and useful in the modern American economy.

Notes

[1] U.S. House of Representatives, *1969 Listing of Operating Federal Assistance Programs Compiled During the Roth Study,* 91st Congress, First session (1969). See also U.S. Congress, Joint Economic Committee, *Subsidy and Subsidylike Programs of the U.S. Government,* Joint Committee Print, 86th Congress, Second session (1960).

[2] This section is condensed from Robert Eyestone, "The Life Cy-

cle of American Public Policies: Agriculture and Labor Policy Since 1929," paper presented at the annual meeting of the Midwest Political Science Association, 1968.

[3] Charles O. Jones, "Representation in Congress: The Case of the House Agriculture Committee," *American Political Science* Review 55 (1961): 358–67.

[4] Lloyd D. Musolf, *Government and the Economy* (Chicago: Scott, Foresman, 1965), pp. 168–69.

[5] *Government and the Economy,* p. 32.

[6] Marver H. Bernstein, *Regulating Business by Independent Commission* (Princeton, N.J.: Princeton University Press, 1955). See also Samuel P. Huntington, "The Marasmus of the ICC," *Yale Law Journal* LXI (April 1952): 467–81, 492–9.

[7] V. O. Key, Jr., *Politics, Parties and Pressure Groups* (5th ed., New York: Crowell, 1964), pp. 138ff.

5

The Political Dynamics of Economic Management

Federal management or direction is a form of economic intervention intended to supplement or supplant the market in the provision of certain goods and services. Most federal management activities occur in areas where the market is obviously an inadequate provider—that is, areas of "public goods." There are few instances of direct federal competition with private producers, and such competition is generally considered inappropriate.

Aside from national defense, which is traditionally a national public function, the largest dollar volume of federal management expenditures occurs in compulsory unemployment and retirement insurance under Social Security. Programs like the TVA, which does compete with private power companies, have been controversial and infrequent. Another example of federal economic management, the interstate highway system, is not controversial because it does not compete with private profit-making activities. Instead it competes with state and county roads, which are not profit-making enterprises because the user taxes that finance them cannot legally be used for any purpose other than road construction.

The primary federal management responsibility, assurance

of national economic prosperity, has also become the most controversial one in recent years. Some of the controversy surrounding taxation and expenditure, the chief instruments of national economic management, has been inevitable. As total expenditure levels increase, financing becomes more difficult because the revenue which must be raised usually increases as a percentage of national income, squeezing taxpayers harder every year. In addition to this built-in problem, counter-cyclical policy constraints on aggregate taxation and spending levels have added more problems for policy makers. Budgetary principles require expenditures to be determined by program needs, and tax levels to be set so as to cover expenditures, irrespective of the state of the economy. Counter-cyclical fiscal policy, on the other hand, requires a net budget surplus of revenues over expenditures when economic conditions are inflationary and a net deficit when the economy is sluggish. These two standards often conflict with each other, and this conflict gives rise to the intense political battles waged over appropriation and tax bills almost every year.

In the 1960s three full-scale tax battles took place: the tax cut of 1964, the surtax of 1968, and the tax reform bill of 1969. In each case, although the conflict was ostensibly about tax rates, questions of spending levels and priorities were also involved. These three cases provide clear examples of an open, public national level economic policy decision—pattern C of Chapter 3—but even here the interests of individual economic sectors have their effect, so that pattern B might be a more appropriate description. To see how and why system and sector level interests can each be expressed in fiscal policy, it is first necessary to look at the policy makers themselves in greater detail.

Making Decisions to Tax and Spend

The cast of characters in tax policy includes several executive agencies, several congressional committees, and a number of private economic interest groups. In the executive branch the

President's Council of Economic Advisers assesses the state of the economy and recommends to the President appropriate fiscal policies to achieve desired levels of economic growth, employment, price stability, and balance of international payments. At the same time the Bureau of the Budget (since 1970 the Office of Management and Budget) is assembling the appropriations requests from the various federal departments and attempting to fit them into Presidential priorities and aggregate spending level guidelines. The CEA's economic policy recommendations, as modified by the President, become part of the *Economic Report of the President,* delivered to Congress at the beginning of each year. The OMB's efforts become the budget the President submits to Congress at about the same time each year.

In accordance with the Employment Act of 1946, the *Economic Report* is considered by the Joint House-Senate Committee on the Economic Report, more commonly called the Joint Economic Committee. What this committee does with the report is not entirely clear, since the report is not in itself a request for congressional action. If the *Economic Report* calls for increased public housing expenditure, for example, Congress need not commit itself for or against this recommendation until it receives a specific budget request to that effect (a request for appropriations under an existing program) or until a bill is introduced that calls for a new housing program (a new authorization request).

Ideally the *Economic Report* serves as the macroeconomic rationale for specific federal programs, and it is in this light that the Joint Economic Committee usually reviews the report. If the committee wishes to make recommendations to Congress formally, they will take the form of resolutions voted on by the House and Senate. The hearings themselves are published and available to every congressman, of course, and there is also undoubtedly a lot of informal communication between the Joint Economic Committee members and their colleagues in both houses. Through these means, then, the President's view is transmitted to the Congress and the views of Congress are made known to the President.

In recent years the Joint Economic Committee has become increasingly bureaucratized, developing a number of specialized subcommittees to carry out spade work and hold background hearings on subjects not directly related to the President's Report—cost overrides in defense contracting, for example.[1] These hearings may give rise to specific legislative proposals. Some of this expansion of the JEC's activities reflects the predilections of the committee's members, especially its chairman, Senator William Proxmire (D., Wisconsin). Proxmire has been a persistent and sensible critic of waste in federal spending, and it is largely at his instigation that the committee has delved into federal contracting and accounting practices. Other committee work, such as its extensive 1966 hearings on the economic impact of the Vietnam war,[2] follows quite naturally from the committee's general responsibilities.

Changes in tax law, including Social Security changes, are expressed in bill form and considered by the Ways and Means Committee in the House and by the Finance Committee in the Senate. Tax rate revision does not occur on a set timetable, as spending decisions do, but irregularly on executive request because most tax measures are drafted for indefinite periods. Since World War II, however, Congress has shown a strong tendency to treat expressly counter-cyclic tax rate changes as temporary measures, to be approved for only one or two years at a time.

Federal expenditure proposals are considered by the Appropriations Committees in the House and Senate. These are probably the most effective, and in the case of the House, the most specialized of the committees in Congress. The House Appropriations Committee has a number of standing subcommittees that consider the requests from the various departments each year. Each subcommittee, because of repeated exposure to the departments within its purview, develops considerable familiarity with the departments' programs, needs, difficulties, and past performance. The subcommmittees focus on changes in appropriation requests from year to year, applying a skeptical budget-cutting approach to requests for unusually large increases. The Senate Appropriations Committee is more generous, often restoring some of the cuts made in the House and necessitating compromise in the House-Senate conference committee.[3]

At no time does congressional procedure require an official meeting or formal agreement between the taxation committees and the expenditure committees. Any coordination between the two sides of the budget must take place through informal cooperation among congressmen or through coordination in the executive branch.

Fortunately, the executive branch speaks with one voice most of the time. The Director of the Office of Management and Budget, the Chairman of the Council of Economic Advisers, and the Secretary of the Treasury appear at congressional hearings as supporting spokesmen for executive budgetary and tax requests, regardless of any differences and doubts they may hold in private. Only in rare instances is the facade of unity broken in public, but the consequences of a break can be disastrous. In 1957, for example, on the day the new budget went to Congress, Eisenhower's Treasury Secretary George Humphrey held an extraordinary press conference in which he warned that the new budget would cause a recession "that would curl your hair" unless it was cut substantially. This comment played right into the hands of congressional economizers, and Eisenhower unfortunately compounded his problems by admitting that he was uneasy about the level of spending proposed in the budget. In fact he went so far as to direct the Budget Bureau to make cuts in the budget already presented to Congress. The way was then clear for major inroads on the President's programs.[4]

A more common pattern of disagreement pits the President's fiscal policy advisers against the Federal Reserve Board (the "Fed"). The reasons for disagreement are obvious—each party in carrying out its own responsibilities may cause problems for the other. William McChesney Martin, Chairman of the Federal Reserve Board from 1955 to 1970, did not hesitate to decry executive "fiscal irresponsibility" when it strained the Fed's capacity to prevent inflationary economic growth.

Presidents, for their part, may bring indirect pressure to bear on the Federal Reserve Board when the political consequences of tight money begin to outweigh the political costs of inflation. A common technique is for the President to encourage a member of his Cabinet—the Secretary of Labor or the Secretary of Housing and Urban Development for example—to publicly criticize some of the adverse effects of Fed policy and to suggest appropriate policy modifications. Pressure of this sort is not always effective, however. In January 1966, for example, the Fed braved presidential objections to raise the discount rate sharply, leading to the "credit crunch" of 1966. Success in changing monetary policy through executive pressure may not be crucial for the President in the long run anyway, since open Presidential criticism helps to shift blame away from the President and members of his administration and his party.

Taxing and Spending: Politics as Usual

Some of the comments just made hint at the "hidden" politics of economic policy, and it is time to spell out those political considerations. Strangely enough, the politics of federal taxation and spending, even though they involve a distinctive subject matter, are similar in many respects to the politics of policy making in any other area of federal involvement. They are formed primarily by the differences of responsibility, economic interest, and resulting policy perspective between the executive and legislative branches. Sometimes these differences appear in economic theory, sometimes as priority differences, and sometimes as divergent economic goals, but in each case these differences have clear institutional causes.

Presidents generally get the blame for inflation and recession. They get part of the blame for tax increases and some of the credit for tax cuts. Congressmen generally get credit for specific spending programs that benefit specific constituencies, regardless of the possibly inflationary effects of total spending. They also receive partial credit for tax cuts and partial blame for tax increases. Thus there is often a conflict between presidential desires to manipulate budget totals in accordance with Keynesian economic theory and congressional requests for various spending programs that benefit their constituents.

Presidents and congressmen like to increase Social Security benefit levels and cut taxes in election years, other things being equal, and they usually cooperate in deferring tax increases until the next election is safely past. When faced with a Presidential request for a tax increase, however, congressmen may press for expenditure cuts instead, apparently feeling that tax hikes are more detrimental politically than a package of spending cuts. Similarly, congressmen do not necessarily need to believe in the Keynesian economic theory which generally guides executive economic policy. Keynesian prescriptions are not relevant to the problems that Congress implicitly takes as its own special responsibility: the impact of taxation and spending on specific sectors and economic interests. Thus whether congressmen really believe in modern economics is often immaterial. The more important question is how much it is necessary for Presidents to promise before Congress will accept their economic policy requests.

Generally speaking, Presidents have to promise, or demonstrate, that the constituency interests of congressmen will not be harmed, that they will be harmed only in ways generally invisible, or at worst that they will be harmed only in equitable ways that can be given broad national justifications. Strong inflationary pressures or war financing needs might constitute cases where tax and spending policy changes can be justified, but only if Congress is convinced that the general public views the proposed measures as absolutely necessary. Usually it would take more work for a President to justify a tax hike or a spending cut on the basis of balance of payments needs than on the basis of inflation or war financing. In these matters congressmen seem to take an almost personal view of the legislative/executive separation of powers, insisting that the executive make some sacrifices just as the legislature is doing. Thus a combination of tax cuts and tax reforms, tax increases and spending cuts, or some other compromise plan, is a frequent outcome of economic policy making.

Beyond these general observations, the constituency interests, and hence the politics of each specific proposal, vary so much that generalizations cannot easily be made. It is possible, however, to examine some cases that bear out the conclusions expressed above and demonstrate how these characteristics of economic policy politics work in specific examples.

The Kennedy Tax Cut

The tax cut proposed in the Kennedy Administration is one such example of Presidential initiative and congressional response. It also illustrates some of the intricacies of politics within the executive branch itself.

That tax cut, eventually passed in 1964 under President Johnson, was the result of several proposals drafted by Kennedy's Council of Economic Advisers chaired by Walter Heller.[5] In principle it was pure Keynesianism, although the Council attempted to move beyond the Keynesian focus on antirecession policies to a more growth-oriented approach. Throughout 1961–63 unemployment was running over 5 percent, and in the small 1961 recession it approached 7 percent. The corresponding loss in annual GNP, compared with its potential at a target unemployment figure of 4 percent, ranged up to $50 billion.

Tax reduction was only part of a sophisticated package of economic management devices proposed by Kennedy's Council of Economic Advisers. The Council's report for 1962 presents the rationale for these devices, many of them intended to be permanent parts of the executive arsenal. Included were investment credits and accelerated depreciation schedules for business, standby authority for executive tax cuts and capital improvements expenditures, and a strengthened unemployment compensation system.

During the 1961 recession the Council urged Kennedy to ask

for a quick tax cut, but Kennedy appeared to be dissuaded from this plan by Treasury Secretary C. Douglas Dillon, who expressed concern about the already unbalanced budget. Kennedy also seems to have been concerned about his campaign theme of "sacrifice" and the apparent incongruity of cutting taxes in the first year of his Presidency. Other events, including the Berlin crisis, intervened in 1961 and most of the Council's economic program was deferred until 1962.

The Berlin crisis, with its demands for increased military spending, temporarily clouded the tax policy picture. By the summer of 1961 President Kennedy had tentatively decided on a $3 billion "Berlin surtax" and he had received support for this plan from within the executive branch. Treasury Secretary Dillon approved of it as a budget-balancing move, and Senator Robert Kennedy though it fit well with the campaign theme of sacrifice. Foreign policy advisers thought it would clearly express American determination in Berlin. Only the President's economic advisers, and Theodore Sorenson, opposed the plan, but they were able to persuade Kennedy not to request the surtax. One of the results of this persuasive effort, though, was Kennedy's determination to balance the budget for fiscal 1962, even as the Berlin military buildup had pushed the probable deficit beyond $6 billion.

In 1962 Congress did pass the investment tax credit and accelerated depreciation programs, and these together with the Berlin spending pulled the economy out of the 1961 recession. The proposals for Presidential standby spending and tax-cutting powers were not well received by Congress, in large part because they trespassed on traditional congressional prerogatives. Congress insisted on its central position in tax rate decision making, just as it insisted on handling "capital improvements" through the congressional pork barrel where the benevolence of Congress could be most clearly appreciated by local constituents. Thus these innovations went by the boards, and President Kennedy had to fall back on a direct request for tax rate cuts. By the summer of 1962, when it became clear that the recovery would not carry the economy all the way to full employment, the tax cut again became a live option.

Into 1963, however, Kennedy encountered opposition to the tax cut from several directions. Some of his personal advisers advocated spending increases instead of tax cuts to meet some of the country's pressing domestic needs. His cabinet reacted strongly against tax cuts of any kind, as did many congressmen and most of the general public. The Heller version of Keynesian doctrine, emphasizing future growth in the economy, had not previously been offered to the public or to Congress and neither of these two accepted the idea immediately. In the popular mind, tax cutting inevitably meant further budget deficits regardless of the state of the economy. Even among the more sophisticated congressmen, an economic upturn like that of 1962 seemed like a good time to raise taxes or cut expenditures, or both.

Against these attitudes Kennedy and his economic advisers mounted an educational campaign involving television messages, public appearances and speeches, and the invention of some new "pop economics," especially the concepts of the "unemployment gap" and "fiscal drag." By the end of 1963 these efforts were beginning to show some results, and the tax cut was finally passed in March 1964. In the course of this persuasive effort, however, Kennedy and his advisers sometimes found it politically expedient to hedge their economic arguments with broader promises. Thus the tax cut, it was said, would lead to a balanced budget, budgetary frugality, lessened inflationary pressure, an improved balance of payments, a lower public debt, and even improved race relations. On the other side of the argument, Kennedy hinted in 1963 that failure to pass the tax cut could bring on another recession. Even if true, these promises make concessions to older stereotyped economic thinking, leaving the final "Keynesianizing" of American economic thought as a problem for subsequent Presidents.[6]

The Surtax Controversy, 1967–68

President Johnson's difficulties in passing a surtax were shaped by the mistakes he made in presenting the surtax and working for its passage and by the general political situation in which the surtax was proposed. Combined, these two elements picture a President working in difficult times to get Congress to pass an unpopular program he had himself been reluctant to propose. Both the situation and the mistakes Johnson made in it were important, but perhaps the situation itself was the overriding factor.[7]

Some of President Johnson's mistakes in the surtax case were given official credence long before the surtax was passed; others came to be realized only in the exasperatingly long process of congressional decision making. One of the mistakes recognized very early by Johnson's advisers was the way the surtax was sold to the Congress and the public. For one thing, Johnson's half-hearted commitment to a surtax in early 1967 looked like wavering uncertainty. No congressman will go out on a limb for a wavering and uncertain President, nor will a President convince anyone if he himself does not appear convinced.

The surtax was a difficult concept to sell, and the selling was not done well. In principle a surtax is simple, but in political reality it appears complicated and almost inevitably larger than it actually is. Many taxpayers apparently interpreted a 10 percent surtax as a 10 percent cut in their gross income, where in reality its effect on gross income would not average more than about 3 percent (10 percent surtax multiplied by 30 percent average effective tax rate). The executive branch had to dispel these incorrect interpretations of the surtax before it could be passed, but they do not seem to have devoted much effort to this task until congressional opposition had hardened against the proposal.

Another mistake (of the "fence-mending" variety) concerns the lack of interplay between the White House and the House of Representatives at several points along the line. Communications with Ways and Means Committee Chairman Wilbur Mills (D., Arkansas) had been particularly bad, and the Administration underestimated the seriousness of congressional spending cut sentiment as a result. When spending cuts were finally proposed by the White House, the Appropriations Committee was not always let in on the decision procedure, as had been promised. Congress also apparently did not receive a straight story on the shape of the budget at all times. The budget deficit estimates seemed to ebb and flow as they suited the President's occasion. On top of Johnson's other credibility gap problems, this distorted communication link certainly did not assist the passage of the surtax.

When these mistakes are put in the context of the national political scene in 1967 and 1968, it seems remarkable that a surtax was passed at all. With one exception the factors beyond the control of the President made Johnson's job more difficult. The fortuitous occurrence and recurrence of European monetary difficulties, the only positive factor in the situation, provided the the President with an additional justification for urgency in passing the surtax, but at the same time the monetary crisis posed difficulties of its own for President Johnson.

One of Johnson's main problems was that the economy refused to cooperate. Instead of presenting a picture of rampant and uncontrolled inflation, the economy persisted in generating ambiguous statistics that undercut the Administration's case. The same contradictory economic performance contributed to the fluctuating budget deficit figures and to the initial delay from January 1967, when the surtax (at 6 percent) was first mentioned, until August 1967, when it was officially proposed at 10 percent (see the chronology of events in Figure 2). The slack economic growth, excess plant capacity and low volume of retail sales in 1967 served Wilbur Mills as valuable ammunition in denying the Administration's surtax requests, and they also contributed quite understandably to congressional suspicions that the Johnson Administration was not being entirely honest in its presentation of the need for a surtax.

Until the spring of 1968, the general public seemed to be opposed to higher taxes. Throughout 1967 Gallup polls showed that the President had failed to convince the public that a surtax was needed, and under those conditions it was extremely unlikely that Congress would consent readily to a tax hike. Of course the American public is rarely willing to be taxed, and George Gallup

Figure 2
Chronology of Events in the 1968 Surtax Controversy

January 1967. President Johnson, in his State of the Union message, proposes a 6 percent income surtax to be effective July 1, 1967, contingent upon expected inflationary pressures later in the year. Fiscal 1968 budget envisions a deficit of $8 billion, counting $5 billion of new revenue from the surtax.

June 1967. Following several months of slow economic growth congressional leaders fear that a surtax may be necessary to make up for revenue shortage considerably greater than that anticipated in the January budget, but they also urge spending cuts to further reduce the expected deficit in the 1968 budget.

August 1967. President Johnson officially requests a 10 percent surtax to be effective October 1, 1967. Revised budgetary figures show a $22 billion deficit, including surtax revenue. The House Ways and Means Committee begins hearings on the President's proposal.

October 1967. The House Ways and Means Committee votes to set the surtax proposal aside until "the President and Congress reach an understanding on a means of implementing more effective expenditure reductions and controls."

November 1967. The British government devalues the pound, causing instability in the international money market. The Federal Reserve Board raises its prime rediscount rate in an attempt to restore confidence in the dollar. The House Ways and Means Committee opens new hearings, focusing on spending cuts rather than on the surtax itself. The Johnson Administration promises $2.6 billion in spending cuts, but Ways and Means Chairman Wilbur Mills rejects this level as insufficient.

January 1968. In hearings over the fiscal 1969 budget, the Ways and Means Committee again defers the surtax until more spending reductions are promised. A Gallup poll reports that 79 percent of Americans oppose a surtax.

February 1968. Budget Director Zwick, Treasury Secretary Fowler and Fed Chairman Martin all appear before the Joint Economic Committee to request a surtax. The committee generally recommends that spending cuts be made instead. The House passes a bill continuing excise taxes on telephone bills and automobiles and calling for a speed-up of corporate income tax collections.

March 1968. In Senate Finance Committee hearings on the excise tax measure, Treasury Secretary Fowler asks that the income surtax be passed, in effect urging the Senate to put pressure on the House by

Figure 2 (continued)

attaching the surtax as a rider to the pending excise tax bill. President Johnson announces willingness to cut \$8–9 billion from the 1969 budget. President Johnson announces that he will not run for re-election.

April 1968. The Senate approves a rider to the excise tax bill calling for a 10 percent surtax and a \$6 billion spending cut. The House-Senate conference committee agrees on the excise tax extension but puts aside the surtax rider. Chairman Mahon of the House Appropriations Committee and Chairman Mills of the House Ways and Means Committee confer with each other and with Administration officials about a possible spending cut-surtax package. Congressional leaders of both parties declare that the President must publicly propose a program of spending cuts before any agreement can be reached.

May 1968. An apparent deal between Johnson and Mills, calling for a 10 percent surtax and a \$4 billion spending cut falls through. The House-Senate conference committee agrees on a \$6 billion spending cut provision. Final House vote on the measure is postponed until June.

June 1968. President Johnson reluctantly says he will accept the \$6 billion spending cut. The House and Senate pass the surtax bill and Johnson signs it. Along with increased corporate and personal income taxes and a cut in current spending, the bill also sets a permanent federal employment ceiling and calls for a \$10 billion reduction in pending appropriations requests.

---

probably would have found majority opposition to the surtax even in May of 1968, if he had taken a poll then. More important than public opinion, perhaps, was the sentiment of various interest groups that might figure prominently in congressional campaign financing later in 1968. It is significant that organized labor never did approve of the surtax. In the spring of 1968 the Johnson Administration did succeed in neutralizing the effect of labor opposition, however, by persuading labor lobbyists to remain silent on the tax issue.

Initially the business community does not seem to have been convinced of the need for a surtax, as Fed Chairman Martin revealed in congressional testimony late in 1967. By 1968 many business groups seem to have come around to a position of acceptance, if not enthusiasm, for a tax increase as a result of persuasive efforts on the part of Johnson Administration spokesmen.

President Johnson had his own partisan political problems with the surtax, which were not completely resolved until he announced in March 1968 that he would not run for reelection. In 1967 and 1968 he was being strongly challenged within the party by peace candidate Eugene McCarthy and later by Robert Kennedy. This challenge made Johnson unwilling to request the surtax specifically to finance the Vietnam war, but at the same time it made the spending cuts demanded by Congress even more difficult than they normally would be. On the "wartax" issue, which many congressmen seemed willing to accept, Johnson could be criticized by Democratic doves because of public ambivalence toward the war. If he cut domestic spending, on the other hand, Johnson's actions would seem to confirm the charge that he was financing the war at the expense of the poor in the United States. Johnson's withdrawal from the Presidential race removed the personal political element from the surtax controversy, but the basic issue of priorities remained unsolved.

The surtax is a classic example of the maxim, "The President proposes, but Congress disposes." A central element in the political dynamics of the case is congressional motivation. Why was the House, and Wilbur Mills especially, so set in opposition to the surtax? What did they stand to gain by delaying what was probably an inevitable measure?

An explanation of the motives of Congress begins with the observation that whenever the President says "tax rate changes" the Congress responds "spending cuts" or "tax reform." The regularity of these responses and the fact that they don't always make economic sense lead one to suspect that they come from differences in the institutions themselves rather than reflecting the circumstances behind any particular Presidential request. The House of Representatives jealously guards its constitutional prerogatives in the areas of taxation and spending. Wilbur Mills in his tenure as

Chairman of the House Ways and Means Committee has doggedly resisted any attempts by the executive to gain more freedom from congressional fiscal control.

Since the Congress no longer actually originates revenue and expenditure bills, its only fiscal power lies in response and reaction to Presidential initiatives. This being the case, the best way to preserve congressional leverage over Presidential economic policy is by exercising congressional prerogatives at every possible opportunity. If in this process congressmen can also reap some political rewards through modifications of tax legislation aimed at narrow constituency interests, so much the better. For Wilbur Mills, though, the primary consideration is certainly protecting the congressional "power of the purse" just as the House Appropriations Committee seeks to "protect the Treasury" from the profligate spenders in the executive departments.[8]

A corollary of this interpretation is that Presidential success, meaning success for economic policy oriented toward national system-level goals and effects, will depend on the general state of the relations of the President to Congress at any given moment. Presidential strengths and weaknesses in other policy areas will affect the President's ability to push his economic policy requests through Congress since there is nothing to insulate economics from other policy areas once these requests get to Congress. If President Johnson had attempted to pass a surtax in 1965, when Congress was strongly Democratic and was passing nearly every measure Johnson proposed, he almost certainly would have had an easier time than in 1967, when Congress was generally less receptive to Presidential requests, when the credibility gap had begun to open over Vietnam, when urban violence seemed to point toward a failure in the War on Poverty, and when Johnson was being strongly challenged for leadership of his own party.

With these explanations in mind, we can identify one further reason why Wilbur Mills may have wanted to delay the surtax. Mills is a man of high seniority and a respected figure in the House. Over the years he has built up a reputation for competence and has been remarkably successful in shepherding tax measures through House floor debate. He has compiled this enviable record by working hard for unity on his committee, never committing himself prematurely on an issue, and never bringing a bill to the full House until he is sure it has enough votes to pass.[9] Ability to delay a measure in committee is invaluable for all three of these purposes. In the surtax case it was especially easy for Mills to delay because he could criticize the Administration's economic interpretations in addition to demanding spending cuts and tax reform.

Of course nothing that has been said here is meant to imply that Mills was insincere in his delaying tactics. In 1968 he did succeed in stalling the surtax until the economic necessity for it was clear, and he did start a tax reform movement which his committee later passed under the Nixon Administration. (The tax reform proposals required as part of the Revenue and Expenditure Control Act of 1968 formed the basis for the Nixon Administration proposals which became part of the Tax Reform Act of 1969.) A more accurate interpretation is simply that the politics of Mills' leadership position in the House coincided with his own economic views and those of many of his fellow congressmen.

The Sector Impact of Taxation

In addition to open conflict over taxing and expenditure levels, a second pattern in governmental economic management arises from the sector level impact of the taxes needed to finance federal spending and to guide the economy. Here the political dynamics are quite similar to those displayed by federal subsidization. The Treasury Department, in its constant concern for taxing power sufficient to cover federal revenue needs, espouses a general policy of fair—meaning equal—tax burdens. Congress, on the other hand, is responsive to a variety of pleas for special tax treatment and exemptions, just as it is responsive to requests for special subsidies through direct spending programs. A pattern of "exceptions politics" emerges in which the basic tax rates for individual income and corporate income are riddled with a number of exemptions, exclusions, and other "loopholes" through which many billions of dollars of income can legally escape taxation each year.

Some of these exemptions can be defended on grounds of fairness, or equity—they impose unequal tax burdens, but only in recognition of the different economic situations of various people. The standard $650 personal exemption, for example, recognizes that wage earners of comparable income may differ widely in their irreducible subsistence expenditures because of differences in family size.

Other exemptions can only be called subsidies-in-disguise. They have no possible equity justification, but are instead intended to encourage an economic sector interest which is generally held to be desirable or which has political power sufficient to gain such a subsidy. The 7 percent investment tax credit extended to business at various times in the 1960s is an example of a non-equitable tax break which serves the purpose of encouragement of economic growth through partial federal subsidization of business investment spending.

The federal tax laws harbor both equitable and subsidy tax breaks in great numbers, and the Treasury is largely unsuccessful in fighting against either variety of loophole. The Treasury loses these battles for a variety of reasons.[10] In thc first place, it is a lone defender of tax equity facing a number of special interests, each with an equity argument for modifications in the labyrinthine tax laws. Second, Treasury pleas are not well received in Congress. Congressmen on the tax committees are generally more sympathetic to their constituents, and the constituents of other congressmen, than they are to the Treasury and its concern for relatively abstract principles of equity. In turn, because members of the House Ways and Means Committee and the Senate Finance Committee can grant specific tax exemptions, they enjoy bargaining advantages in dealings with all other congressmen who might have groups seeking special tax favors among their constituents. These bargains among congressmen, whether implicit or explicit, may increase the chance of success for tax bills or enhance the influence of tax committeemen in nontax areas.

In short, members of the tax committees benefit from nearly absolute control of the subject matter of their committees, just as members of the agriculture committees, for example, profit by their control over agriculture and related policies. With the exceptions of the appropriations and foreign relations committees, the tax committees probably confer the greatest advantages on their members of any of the committees in Congress because of the breadth of tax policy impact.

A third and central part of the "exceptions politics" pattern displayed by tax loopholes is the public invisibility of the process. Individually, tax loopholes and special exemptions are simply not newsworthy, nor do they often excite the average taxpayer, who has to foot the bill for them in the end. A genuine "taxpayers' revolt" such as that alleged to have occurred in 1969 is a rare phenomenon in American politics, although tax reform is a perennial promise that either party stands ready to make if it should prove politically advantageous. But as long as little criticism is generated by each specific loophole in the tax laws, public emotions do not become sufficiently aroused to create an undeniable demand for overall tax reform.

The taxpayers' revolt of 1969, if there was such a thing, was popularized by revelations of relatively rare situations such as the several hundred millionaires who escaped taxation entirely. Cases of this type, while unquestionably involving large sums of tax money, probably have more symbolic than monetary significance. To the average taxpayer, the thought that the government must collect several hundred million dollars extra in taxes from the middle class is probably not as galling as the thought that a few people escaped legally without paying any taxes at all.

The symbolic aspect of the public reaction to tax loopholes provided an easy course of action for Congress in its tax reform deliberations in 1969. Since the scot-free few were such a visible target of resentment, it was easy to apply a minimum tax rate to all income for persons who might otherwise report no net income subject to taxes. At the same time, though, the minimum rate could be set quite low because the dollar amount of escaping taxes was not very important politically. Thus the final provisions of the tax reform package passed late in 1969 included a 10 percent tax on most forms of tax-free income in excess of $30,000.

The logic of the tax exceptions procedure often leads Congress into the ludicrous position of passing a tax bill so overburdened with special provisions as to invite Presidential veto. Once the validity of any special claim is allowed there is no way of denying other special claims, especially since each claim is pushed by a fellow congressman on behalf of someone in his constituency.

In recent years the Senate Finance Committee has been particularly prone to this practice, perhaps because it views itself as a kind of appellate body for requests which have received harsh treatment in the House. In 1966 and again in 1969 the Senate passed tax measures which were widely referred to as "Christmas Tree" bills because of the large number of special provisions introduced into each one at the last minute. As Chairman Russell Long (D., Louisiana) expressed it, the 1966 bill was "the last train out of the station"—the last chance for any stalled special favors tax legislation for the 1966 session.[11] Among the bill's provisions were a special extension of the investment tax credit for a new aluminum plant in the Virgin Islands, higher depletion allowances for mineral-bearing clay in Georgia and Arkansas (favored by senators from Georgia and Arkansas), lowering of taxes on the importation of J&B Scotch, and an excise tax cut on hearses.[12]

In 1969 the Senate added over seventy specific provisions to the Tax Reform Act of 1969, which had already been passed by the House. Many of them, such as the amendments introduced by Senator Cooper (R., Kentucky) benefiting horse farms and coal mines and the amendment introduced by Senator Bennett (R., Utah) benefiting Litton Industries, had definite and specific targets far removed from the general reform thrust of the bill. In this case it is possible that the senators had their cake and ate it too. They knew that the bill they passed would have to go to a House-Senate conference committee and that many of the Senate amendments would be dropped in order to reach a final compromise. By thus overloading the bill with special provisions they might please their constituents and at the same time not prejudice the bill's overall purpose because many of the specific exceptions they made in the bill would never become law.

When tax exceptions get as far out of hand as they did in the 1966 and 1969 Senate bills, they cannot remain completely isolated from national level considerations. In 1969, for example, between Senate action and the House-Senate conference committee President Nixon became sufficiently concerned about the effects on the national economy of expanded Social Security payments, increased personal exemptions and the variety of special tax favors volunteered by the Senate that he threatened to veto the bill if he received it in essentially the form passed by the Senate. When the conference responded to this pressure by restoring $6 billion in lost taxes out of the $9 billion that the President wanted, Nixon decided that the bill merited signature.

Economic Management: To What Effect?

The impact of federal economic management is difficult to measure or express precisely because it has ramifications in a number of areas. In this section it is possible to review briefly only a few of the aggregate effects of federal taxation and spending.

One federal policy whose effects are commonly misunderstood is deficit financing. Under wartime and depression conditions, the federal government has often engaged in deficit spending—that is, it has borrowed to pay for some current expenses instead of taxing. Economists generally agree that government borrowing, to the extent that it supplements rather than replaces private borrowing, contributes to the growth of national income.

Each dollar of deficit spending that government borrowing makes possible creates several dollars in increased national income because of the multiplier effect resulting from purchases by the initial recipients of the government spending.

Thus the current national debt of more than $300 billion that is owed by one group of Americans to another group of Americans may perhaps have contributed as much as $1,000 billion to our total of national income over the years, enough wealth to construct 20,000 good-sized office buildings or to fill the current poverty gap in the United States fifty times. Of course, not all of the wealth generated by such internal borrowing is immediately available for the pursuit of public goals since much of it falls into private hands via the consumer spending of Federal employees and other direct beneficiaries of deficit spending. Only by taxation can this "multiplier" income be tapped for public spending.[13]

Before we give our enthusiastic approval to unbalanced federal budgets, we should weigh the inflationary pressures budget deficits can create in an already prosperous economy against the possible increases in national wealth that deficit financing can bring about. Price inflation is not in itself dangerous to the economy, but it is inequitable in the burdens it places on various classes of income earners. The union man whose leaders bargain aggressively for him does not need to fear inflation because his wages will generally keep ahead of inflationary changes in the economy. For persons on fixed incomes, however, inflation represents a real cut in living standard. Retired persons living on savings, annuities, or Social Security, as well as many public employees accustomed to receiving small and infrequent pay raises, all suffer under inflation. In the first case the effects of inflation are markedly unfair; in the second case they may also undermine the quality of public services because local police and fire departments and federal bureaus alike may not be able to offer wages competitive with those in private employment.[14]

A second major class of effects of federal economic management, and an important secondary management purpose, revolves around the impact of federal taxing and spending on the distribution of income in the society. Aside from "pure public goods" like national defense, from which everyone benefits equally, nearly every federal expenditure program represents a transfer of wealth to some specific category or group within the population. The Model Cities program, for example, sends funds directly into the core areas of large cities for the purposes of planning and rehabilitation in accordance with the wishes of core area residents. Farm price supports directly benefit the small (and diminishing) proportion of Americans engaged in agriculture. When these programs are financed by a system of taxes that draws revenue from the population in a differential manner, it is obvious that federal fiscal activities have the potential for very powerful income redistribution over and above their uses in maintaining aggregate economic prosperity.

The federal personal income tax incorporates income redistribution in its rate structure by seeking to place tax burdens where there is an "ability to pay." Above a minimum level of income, increasingly higher marginal tax rates are applied as taxable income increases until some maximum tax bracket is reached. In 1969, for example, the lowest marginal rate was 14 percent, for taxable income under $1,000; the highest was 70 percent, for all taxable income over $200,000 on joint returns. For all taxing units with any net taxable income, then, the structure of federal income tax rates is progressive. For taxing units with no net taxable income, the rate structure is not progressive.

To illustrate this point, consider a typical family of two adults and two children. In 1969 this family would have no net taxable income if it earned less than $3,000 ($2,400 in personal exemptions and $600 for the standard deduction), thus it would pay the same tax—zero—for any level of gross income from zero to $3,000 a year. Ironically, the provisions of the Tax Reform Act of 1969 make the rate structure *less* progressive in the sense that they raise the point at which marginal tax rates begin to apply. By 1973 the same family of four will have no net taxable income until it earns $3,600 ($3,000 for personal exemptions and $600 for the standard deduction).

Of course, the rate structure does not tell the whole story.

The marginal rates apply to net taxable income, which is less than gross income by the total of exemptions, deductions, credits, and the like applying to any given individual taxpayer's earnings. A more revealing figure is the effective tax rate, which is simply the total tax liability expressed as a percentage of gross income. Table 4 shows the median effective tax rates, the maximum effective rates, and the estimated range of effective rates on actual returns for 1969. It is clear from these data that much of the progressive character of the income tax has been eroded by special tax treatment granted to various kinds of income.

The effective tax rates provide plenty of ammunition for tax reformers in that most of the advantages of tax "loopholes" fall to the upper middle class and the very wealthy taxpayers. Effective tax rates are also highly unequal: the tax take varies widely for any level of gross income, from those who exempt virtually all their income from taxation to the few who claim only the minimum personal exemptions and standard deductions.

For the lowest income brackets, the variations in effective rate for taxpayers with similar gross incomes depends mainly on

Table 4
Estimated Effective Tax Rates, 1969

Gross income category	*Maximum effective tax rate*	*Median effective tax rate*	*Range of effective rates*
0–$3,000	16%	3%	0–16%
$3,000–$5,000	16	15	0–16
$5,000–$7,000	16	16	0–16
$7,000–$10,000	18	17	0–18
$10,000–$15,000	23	17	0–23
$15,000–$20,000	28	18	0–28
$20,000–$50,000	44	21	0–44
$50,000–$100,000	55	30	0–55
$100,000–$500,000	67	32	0–67
$500,000–$1,000,000	68	27	0–68
Over $1,000,000	70	26	0–70

Source: Office of the Secretary of the Treasury, Office of Tax Analysis, cited in Joseph W. Barr, "Tax Reform: The Time Is Now," *Saturday Review* (March 22, 1969), p. 23.

the number of personal exemptions claimed by the taxpayer. A single person with a gross income of $6,000 would have paid $866 in taxes in 1969, for example, while a person claiming five dependents would have been liable for only $230 on $6,000 of income. Extremes like these are uncommon, however, and the actual effective rates for the low and middle income brackets cluster remarkably. For each of the income groups between $3,000 and $20,000, more than 60 percent of the taxpayers paid effective rates between 15 and 20 percent in 1969.

For the higher income brackets the personal exemption fades in importance but other forms of deduction become significant. The favorite loopholes for high income taxpayers—exemption of half of long-term capital gains, the tax exempt status of most state and municipal bonds, and the mineral depletion allowances such as that applying to oil—generally require large investments and are therefore unavailable to low and middle income taxpayers. One consequence of the variety of loopholes applicable at high income levels is a marked inequity in tax rate. Over the range between $20,000 to $500,000 there is almost no tendency for effective rates to cluster.

In short, how you earn your income has a major impact on how much you pay in taxes. Thus for a broad middle and upper income range the tax structure provides a strong incentive away from salary income and toward various forms of investment. Taxpayers who respond to this incentive retain much more of their income after taxes than taxpayers who do not (or can not).

"Loophole" is a loaded word. One man's loophole may be another man's tax equity, or as congressmen say, his sacred constitutional prerogative. To get around these semantic difficulties we can refer to all such tax breaks as "tax expenditures." Viewed dispassionately, tax breaks can be seen to fall to both the rich and the poor. The poor do not benefit from tax expenditures as much in sheer dollar terms as the rich, but then the rich *do* have more income to begin with.

Viewing loopholes as tax expenditures also points to the kind of effect they have on the economy. As far as changes in the quantity of various kinds of private economic activity are concerned, tax expenditures are exactly equivalent to direct subsidies. When the Treasury does not collect tax money because of private spending for some specific exempted purpose, it is just as if the tax had been collected and then paid back as a subsidy for the earmarked purpose. The activity in question is encouraged by being made more profitable than it would otherwise have been.

The aggregate size of tax expenditures is very large, in some cases considerably larger than direct budgetary outlays for related purposes. Table 5 shows estimates of budgetary and tax expenditures for fiscal 1970. In each of the four areas, tax breaks are enjoyed by all income groups.[15] In education, for example, wealthy taxpayers benefit from the deductibility of contributions to educational institutions, while the less wealthy benefit from the tax-free status of scholarships and fellowships. Health "expenditures" are swelled by the extra aged and blind exemptions, dependent medical care deductibility and the sick pay exclusion, among others. Homeowners enjoy favored tax status in the deductibility of property taxes and mortgage interest. Builders of rental housing are subsidized by excess depreciation allowances against rental income, but indirectly renters themselves benefit from this subsidy because it increases the supply of new rental housing and tends to hold down the level of rental rates on new apartments. The tax expenditure represented by the exclusion of

Table 5
Budget Outlays and Tax Expenditures, Fiscal 1970
(in billions of dollars)

Programs	*Budget outlays*	*Tax expenditures*
Education and manpower	7.9	0.9
Health and welfare	55.0	19.5
Commerce and transportation	9.0	9.7
Community development and housing	2.8	5.2
Total	74.7	35.3

stock dividends is important mainly to small investors because of the $100 yearly limit on such exclusion.

Not even the most dedicated of tax reformers would propose that all of these tax breaks be reformed out of existence, but the problem is one of establishing a balance between the social purposes served by tax exemptions and a possible weakening of the government's taxing ability through erosion of the tax base. Concern over the strength or weakness of the federal tax base stems, of course, from a desire to maintain the federal government's ability to finance a broad range of foreign and domestic programs. Since budgetary outlays and tax expenditures are interchangeable as far as the beneficiaries, and the Treasury, are concerned, the logical solution is to end all tax expenditures and use the increased tax take to finance direct subsidies in the same areas.

Unfortunately, this logical solution does not stand the test of political practicality. In the first place, Americans by conviction seem to resist "government handouts." A tax break serving the same purpose is quite acceptable, however, since the government really doesn't "deserve" all that tax money anyway. Second, and at least as important, tax expenditures are less visible to the general public. Because of their relative invisibility, tax breaks are much less subject to public criticism and attack than would be budgetary outlays of the same size for the same purpose. The effects of political visibility are probably enhanced by the kinds of purposes that are served through tax expenditures, many of which are considered socialistic by large numbers of Americans. Thus many of the purposes furthered by tax breaks probably could not be carried on by direct spending given the persistent tendency of the general public and of some congressmen to resist further government spending—especially federal spending and especially for social programs. Only recently, for example, has the federal government begun a substantial program of direct rent subsidies. Until it becomes possible politically to carry out similar social purposes through direct budgetary outlays, the indirect (and inequitable) device of tax expenditures may be the most practical method available.

The politics of economic management finally lead to another kind of inequity in the impact of tax policy. The slowness with which changes in tax rates and aggregate spending levels can be accomplished throws an undue burden on those management devices that can be changed with less difficulty politically, but whose effects are also less equitable. In the 1960s (in addition to monetary restraint exercised by the Federal Reserve Board), investment tax credits, excise taxes on automobiles and telephone bills, and user charges for federally aided facilities such as airports have all been varied somewhat arbitrarily when quick tax cuts or tax increases could not be pushed through Congress.

The 7 percent tax credit on business investments, for example, was originally proposed by President Kennedy in 1961 as part of a tax reform package, and was passed in 1962. In 1966 President Johnson and Congress agreed to suspend the credit from October 10, 1966 to January 1, 1968, but early in 1967 President Johnson requested that the suspension be lifted, and the credit became available again on March 10, 1967. Among other things, Johnson's economic advisers were worried that investment would dry up entirely during 1967 because businesses would wait for the resumption of the tax credit in 1968. In 1969 the 7 percent investment tax credit was repealed for the indefinite future as part of President Nixon's anti-inflation efforts.

The inequities involved in squeezing business investment, increasing mortgage rates and continuing "temporary" excise taxes indefinitely as ways of maintaining economic prosperity are not inherent features of federal economic management. They spring, rather, from Presidential desperation in the face of a Congress which is unwilling simply to ratify executive economic policy requests. Until the Congress does grant the President greater latitude in fiscal policy (not likely in the near future), some measure of inequity and arbitrariness will be a common characteristic of federal management attempts through fiscal policy devices.

Notes

[1] Joint Economic Committee, Subcommittee on Economy in Government, *The Acquisition of Weapons Systems,* 91st Congress, 1st and 2nd sessions, 1969 and 1970.

[2] Joint Economic Committee, *Economic Effect of Vietnam Spending,* 90th Congress, 1st session, 1967.

[3] See Richard F. Fenno, Jr., *The Power of the Purse: Appropriations Politics in Congress* (Boston: Little, Brown, 1966).

[4] Richard E. Neustadt, *Presidential Power* (New York: Wiley, 1960), Ch. 4.

[5] This narrative draws heavily on E. Ray Canterbery, *Economics on a New Frontier* (Belmont, Calif.: Wadsworth, 1968).

[6] Walter W. Heller, *New Dimensions of Political Economy* (New York: Norton, 1967), p. 39.

[7] This case study is based on contemporary news reports in the *Wall Street Journal* and *The New York Times.*

[8] The general approach of the Ways and Means Committee is described in Aaron Wildavsky, *The Politics of the Budgetary Process* (Boston: Little, Brown, 1964).

[9] John F. Manley, "The House Committee on Ways and Means: Conflict Management in a Congressional Committee," *American Political Science Review* 59 (December, 1965): 927–39.

[10] Stanley S. Surrey, "The Congress and the Tax Lobbyist—How Special Tax Provisions Get Enacted," *Harvard Law Review* 70 (May, 1957): 1145–82.

[11] George Lardner, Jr., *Washington Post,* December 25, 1966, cited in Congressional Quarterly, Inc., *Congress and the Nation,* Vol. II (Washington, D.C.: Congressional Quarterly, 1969), p. 150.

[12] *Congress and the Nation,* p. 150.

[13] Abba P. Lerner, *Everybody's Business* (East Lansing: Michigan State University Press, 1961), pp. 104–14.

[14] Among other places, this argument is made in John Kenneth Galbraith, *The Affluent Society* (Boston: Houghton Mifflin, 1958).

[15] Haig Babian, "Can Taxes Do More Than Raise Revenue?" *Saturday Review* (March 22, 1969), pp. 30ff.

6

A Scheme for Policy Analysis

Value Choices in Policy Analysis

Policy questions are questions of differing values, and policy decisions are the result of some kind of settlement among people whose preferences are somewhat different. A choice usually satisfies some people more than others because it comes closer to what they wanted than to the wishes of others. At a simpler level everyone faces exactly this problem in questions of personal "policy" choice when he decides how to allocate his spending money. There are many possibilities to choose from, but selecting one excludes the others. Five dollars, for example, could buy a book, tickets to the movies, or a good dinner, or it could earn interest in a savings account. Here the competing values are education, entertainment, satiation, future reward, and so on, although few people would think of their choice in those terms.

Public policy decisions are similar except that the spokesmen for the various values involved are usually distinct and represent distinct constituencies. But just as in the simple illustration above they argue in favor of valued things, such as money; valued states, such as national security; or valued concepts, such as freedom or self-reliance. While public policy choices always involve choices among competing values, however, the values and value priorities that policy makers use in reaching decisions are often implicit and unclear. For the student the effort required to unearth these hidden value premises and priorities will be well repaid by an added understanding of the alternatives that could be chosen.

A knowledge of the politics of economic policy making is a great help in identifying the implicit values in current questions of public policy, but it is not a sufficient base for a critical analysis of policy issues. Policy makers come to their task with their own well-formed value preferences and prejudices—in other words, they prejudge issues. Successful policy analysis must look behind these prejudgments and attempt to discover the original value questions, rather than rely on conclusions already formulated by political partisans.

The kind of policy analysis to be outlined in this chapter, for which these value questions are central, can be called prescriptive analysis. This form of analysis begins with actual proposals and current alternatives, sets aside questions of political feasibility, and attempts to work backward from these alternatives to the relevant value preferences. It asks two questions: What values will be affected by this proposal? What value priorities does this proposal imply?

While prescriptive analysis does deal in value alternatives, it does not in itself attempt to make value choices. Such choices nearly always involve intangible elements which will be weighed differently by each individual who evaluates them. The contribution that analysis can make to value choices is to clarify the alternatives by spelling out exactly what, in fact, is the significance of choosing one alternative rather than another. Thus the ultimate value decision rests with the individual, and some kind of political process must be used—voting, compromise, logrolling, and the like—to add up individual value choices and produce a single solution that will become public policy. If the prescriptive analysis has been careful, however, the analyst's own choice among current alternatives should follow immediately once his choice among the underlying values has been made.

An Example: The ABM Decision

Major policy decisions can be quite complex in the value considerations they embody, and often these value considerations are not directly stated in the actual political debate over the alternatives. A good example of this characteristic of policy choices is the ABM decision made early in 1969. The ostensible disagreement between military spokesmen and their congressional critics was a technical one: Would the antiballistic missile system work? Some senators feared that deployment of Safeguard, even though it was aimed at China rather than Russia, would strain our relations with Russia at a time when movement toward detente seemed possible. In good congressional tradition, the senators were also worried that ABM would be a waste of money. Some felt that its mission was basically an impossible one, while others argued that there were cheaper ways of achieving the same deterrent effect.

Thus the surface issues in the ABM debate were those of economy and effectiveness on the one hand, and national security needs on the other. Beneath the surface of congressional criticism, but openly expressed by newspaper and magazine columnists, were other questions of social and political values as well. Many congressmen were concerned about the money Safeguard would cost, not because the country could not pay the bill, but because they were convinced that the choice was between Safeguard and essential (but equally expensive) domestic welfare and housing programs. For them the question was one of the priorities attached to domestic as against foreign spending. Both might have been necessary, but domestic problems were more pressing at the time than defense needs.

Another implicit congressional division over the ABM separated those who valued civilian control of the military from those who generally trusted the military's estimates of defense needs and appropriate defense policies. This was a question of political values that was of great concern to some Senators because they attributed much of the Vietnam war difficulties to inadequate congressional guidance following the Gulf of Tonkin resolution in

1964, and they feared that the military might again head down the wrong path unless Congress pulled in the reins.

In the ABM example it is obviously impossible to say which factor was the sole determinant of the 51 to 49 favorable vote; undoubtedly each factor contributed something to the final result. It is possible though, as has just been done briefly, to examine the alternatives and spell out the value implications of a "yes" or a "no" vote. Beyond this point every individual must decide for himself which alternative is preferable, as each of the 100 senators did on the antiballistic missile.

Political Economic Prescriptions

In theory, then, a model of prescriptive analysis includes four steps:

1. List the alternatives to be considered;
2. Determine what values will be affected by each proposal, examining the alternatives and observing who supports them and who opposes them;
3. Construct a balance sheet for each proposal, weighing the values favorably affected against the values adversely affected; and
4. Choose the proposal offering the greatest preponderance of favorable effects over unfavorable ones.

As is often the case with ideal models, such a procedure could become very involved and time consuming if it were necessary to complete each step as outlined above. Fortunately, several simplifications can be made when applying this analytic scheme to actual policy decisions. First, most proposals are not made in a vacuum, but in relation to the existing state of public policy. If the ABM had been rejected by the Senate, for example, we would not have been left defenseless. On the contrary, the already high level of military spending contributed to much of the congressional criticism of additional spending requests. Thus the ABM was an increment in relation to the total defense budget, albeit a crucial increment in the eyes of its critics.

Second, policy making itself usually proceeds incrementally.

Figure 3
An ABM Balance Sheet

Advantages	*Disadvantages*
Will enhance national security(?)	Very costly
Will demonstrate confidence in military judgment	Wasteful and ineffective(?)
	Will heighten world tensions(?)
	Will weaken the principle of civilian control of the military
	Will prevent necessary domestic spending

Existing policy is not generally questioned when new proposals are made; rather the new proposals are themselves the major focus of discussion. Even a major proposal like the ABM, for example, did not call forth a reevaluation of our entire defense policy, but was debated largely on its own merits. This kind of continuity in policy greatly simplifies the task of analysis because it means that policy *changes* can be evaluated instead of complete policies. For the ABM, for instance, a rough balance sheet might resemble that shown in Figure 3. Such a balance sheet by itself cannot dictate the correct decision, but it can at least summarize the arguments on both sides as an aid to individual choice.

For economic policy the assumption of incremental change is particularly relevant because of the strong American tendency to view governmental action as "intervention" in normal economic processes. The present state of economic policy is partly a conjunction of economic and political values and partly a compromise between the two. Most changes in this balance, especially in the direction of greater governmental intervention, require considerable justification before they can be accepted as public policy. Changes do take place, of course, partly because of changes in political forces and partly because of changes in the shape of the economy, but they are usually slow changes for which an incremental assumption is highly appropriate.

Finally, the analytic task can be made more explicit because it is limited to only a single area—economic policy. The basic analytic questions then become: what values are advanced by the current state of economic relationships? What new values could be served, or what values could be better served, by a different pattern of governmental intervention? Answers to these two questions provide a justification for particular instances of governmental economic intervention.

Types of Political Economic Situations

If the specific political interests surrounding a given governmental action are set aside for a moment, it becomes possible to describe the complex governmental impact on the American economy by using a surprisingly small number of situation types. Each type is characterized by a unique pattern of private economic activity, with its attendant values, and each gives rise to a typical kind of governmental intervention and the values associated with it.

These situations provide a set of rough guidelines which can be applied to specific policy decisions, again assuming that the political factors associated with a given situation have been temporarily disregarded.

Economic situations that might justify governmental intervention can be distinguished according to whether (a) the private economic activity in question already exists or not, and (b) its effects are (or would be) generally beneficial or harmful from a social viewpoint.

Of course many kinds of individual economic activity will not fall into any of the categories to be outlined in this chapter because their social effects are small or are roughly balanced between pluses and minuses, or because the political power of the people they affect is small. One of the obvious legacies of a laissez faire economic philosophy in the United States is the wide latitude allowed private practices before they become matters of public concern. As earlier chapters demonstrated, this philosophy has in fact been significantly undermined by interventional policy decisions, but its effects can still be seen in popular rhetoric and in a generally "conservative" governmental practice with regard to economic intervention.

Figure 4 summarizes the types of political economic situa-

Figure 4
Types of Political Economic Situations

State of activity	*Social judgment*	*Description of the situation*	*Governmental response*	*Illustrations*
1. Existing	Desirable spillover	Conjunction of social and individual goals	Promotion, encouragement	Patent policy, railroad land grants
2. Existing	Intrinsically desirable	Overriding social goals	Subsidization	Agricultural price supports, small business loans
3. Existing	Undesirable spillover	A "public bad"	Remedial regulation	Food and drug laws, Taft-Hartley emergency strike law
4. Existing	Intrinsically undesirable	Overriding social goals	Eradication	Antipollution laws, antigambling laws
5. Nonexisting: cannot be user charged	Desirable	A "public good"	Public monopoly	National defense, fire and police protection
6. Nonexisting: can be user charged	Desirable	Quasi-public good	Regulated private monopoly	Telephone and other utilities
7. Nonexisting	Undesirable	Overriding social goals	Preventive regulation	Usury laws

tions that are distinguished in this chapter. In each case the situation is first defined by the social judgment regarding a given economic activity, a brief technical description of the situation is given, and these are followed by the typical pattern of governmental response and some illustrative examples.

EXISTING ACTIVITY, DESIRABLE SPILLOVER

In the first situation an existing economic activity has effects on society that are generally regarded as beneficial. Under these circumstances there is a conjunction between social goals and the goals of the persons engaged in that economic activity. These two sets of goals need not, and probably will not, be similar, but they are related in that they can both be advanced by the economic activity in question.

The most effective governmental policy in this situation is promotional, designed to subsidize and encourage the expansion of private economic activity through the dissemination of information, granting of special protection or exemptions from general laws, loan insurance, and the like. Subsidization will be justified when its advantages outweigh the inherent costs of subsidization. Here economic conditions may justify setting aside the normal presumptions of minimal governmental action, or, more often, special economic interests may have enough power to obtain a government subsidy regardless of economic conditions. If, on the other hand, a desirable activity is already being supplied in quantity sufficient to meet society's demand for it then there is no need for a subsidy.

American patent policy is a good example of type 1 promotional activity. It encourages research and invention while at the same time benefiting the inventor because he or his employer is granted exclusive use of the patented invention. Encouragement of inventions was first proposed as a federal policy in Alexander Hamilton's "Report on Manufactures" presented to the Congress in 1791. His proposal, although not elaborated in much detail, apparently called for direct cash rewards to be paid from the federal Treasury to inventors of useful devices. This suggestion, part of a broad scheme of incentives that also envisioned paying the emigration costs of skilled foreign craftsmen, never became part of public policy, although Hamilton's report did firmly establish the principle of federal promotion for native manufacturing.

The utility of a subsidy is not its promise of a cheap solution to a policy problem. Generally the public pays one way or another; either directly, through higher prices for subsidized inefficiency, or indirectly, through shorter supplies of nonsubsidized activities. The virtue of a subsidy lies in its direct and immediate impact on the subsidized activity. In this sense a subsidy can be used to communicate a social demand to producers more clearly than the market mechanism would communicate it, or it can be used to communicate an artificially larger aggregate demand than would be communicated by the summation of individual demands for a given commodity (see the discussion of public goods below). Of course these arguments apply only to subsidies as conscious, open expressions of a public goal, and not to the many special interest subsidies hidden from public view in tax loopholes and the like.

Once a policy of open subsidization has been chosen, however, the choice of techniques is a matter of some concern. Whether one uses direct cash incentives or the granting of patent rights, for example, is important because of the differing side effects of these two techniques. Both will encourage invention because both offer economic rewards to inventors. But under the Hamilton scheme presumably the inventions would be widely available after the inventor received his reward, while under the patent right arrangement there may be a substantial time lag before a new device can be generally used. Thus the patent system may not encourage the diffusion of inventions, and in that sense it may be an imperfect implementation of the policy of encouragement to inventions.

With the growth of large scale federal research and development spending since the end of World War II, further patent problems have arisen that illustrate some additional difficulties in implementing a promotional policy. The question of patent ownership under government contracted research has been a difficult one, especially since it has often involved research work classified for reasons of national security. Usually the government agency contracting for the research has retained the patent right, but occasionally the contracting firm has received the commercial rights to the patent if it appeared that the public would benefit sooner from this procedure than it would from government control of the patent. In the latter case, however, it has been felt necessary to require the contractor to begin commercial use of his patent within three years so that there would be some guarantee of public benefit.[1] This example shows how an imperfect promotional policy can draw the government into further intervention in an attempt to realize promotion's supposed public benefits.

EXISTING, INTRINSICALLY DESIRABLE ACTIVITY

In the second situation, which is similar to the first, an existing economic activity is viewed by society as being intrinsically desirable, quite apart from any direct spillover effects it may have on any group in the population. As in the first case, this situation does not demand governmental action unless it has been decided politically that there is not enough of the economic activity in question, or if such activity is in danger of disappearing because it is becoming economically unprofitable.

If there is an insufficient supply of an intrinsically desirable economic activity then there is a clear conjunction of social and individual goals and a promotional policy response will usually follow. If a given kind of economic activity is in danger of disappearing, however, the situation is one of overriding social goals. Society is saying, in effect, that no matter how unprofitable a given activity may be, it may still be sufficiently desirable socially to be preserved by a policy of subsidization.

The notable example in recent years of a failing enterprise

that has been saved from complete disaster by governmental subsidization is the family farm. It is certain that many family farms would long ago have reverted to nonagricultural uses or have been bought out by large commercial farms without federal farm home loans, crop loans, the soil bank, crop price supports, and other farm programs.

Preservation of the family farm has apparently been accepted as a worthwhile social goal for which the American public is continually willing to pay several billion dollars annually. Secretaries of Agriculture, especially Democrats, have taken strong stands on this question, although both Secretary Orville Freeman (under President Johnson) and Secretary Clifford Hardin (under President Nixon) have also spoken of broader programs of rural renewal that would provide nonfarm jobs in declining farm areas. These programs, too, would probably require government subsidization to begin with.

The farm problem has not been solved because it is basically an economic problem to which political solutions are being applied. The political solutions to date have not been lasting ones because they have dealt with the symptoms of the problem rather than with the problem itself. The symptoms are overproduction and falling prices, while the problem is too many inefficient marginal producers selling in a market characterized by inelastic demand. Large farms are better able to survive in this kind of market by holding down production or switching crops, while the increased production which is the natural reaction of the small single-crop farmer to falling prices only exacerbates the problem.[2]

The classic economic solution to the farm problem is to allow falling prices to drive out marginal producers until the full output can be sold at prices profitable to every remaining producer. This solution has not been implemented as public policy since the 1930s, however, because of our overriding social commitment to the small farmer. Mention could also be made of the PL 480 programs which dispose of farm surpluses abroad, and of the problems that would result if the country's marginal farmers all moved to urban areas to seek new employment, but these possible justifications for our farm policy do not seem as important as our value commitment to the family farm.

A point to be emphasized in this example is that governmental solutions to economic problems, when predicated on overriding social values, are not necessarily cheap solutions. The American public pays to keep farm prices high and it also pays those prices in food products.

Comparison of the patent and agriculture cases brings out a further important distinction. In subsidizing invention, imagining for a moment that Hamilton's plan had been followed, there is no standard that says how much should be spent. No one knows how much invention the country "really needs," but more would always be welcome if the money is available for it. Thus the subsidization of a profitable activity is always (in theory) subject to budgetary controls. It can be cut back in a tight budgetary year and expanded again later. In agriculture, on the other hand, there is a clear standard for expenditures. The program must guarantee a given level of parity because below that level farmers are not getting an adequate return and will not be able to survive. Therefore the subsidization of a dying activity is a less flexible commitment, one not as amenable to budgetary cuts and increases. This sort of budgetary invulnerability strongly affects the politics of agricultural policy described in Chapter 4, enhancing the power of concerned farm interest groups to preserve the status quo in agriculture.

EXISTING ACTIVITY, UNDESIRABLE SPILLOVER

The third situation includes all existing economic activities that have undesirable spillover consequences for society. Such a situation can be described as one of a nonbeneficial public good, or a "public bad." That is to say, it involves an activity that is to someone's immediate advantage and is socially acceptable in itself, but that produces undesirable side effects on many other citizens, whether they wish it or not.

The usual governmental reaction toward such a situation is to exercise remedial regulation designed to minimize the undesirable effects of the activity in question. Since most economic activities are not completely pernicious but produce some mix of beneficial and harmful effects, only a mild form of regulation is called for rather than the complete elimination of the private activity in question.

Take food and drug legislation as an example, including more recent meat inspection, truth in packaging and other consumer protection laws. The basic economic activities here—the development of new drugs and the manufacture of food products—certainly are valuable. Indeed, drug research may be deserving of subsidization or some other form of encouragement. Instead of eliminating these activities completely to avoid possible abuses, governmental policy seeks only to prevent the undesirable side effects that unregulated production might bring. It sets standards of purity and standards of identity, prescribes testing procedures, and conducts tests on its own to be certain that the legal standards provide the public adequate protection.

Regulatory activity of this kind is subject to many limitations, some political (described in Chapter 4), and some resulting from a chronic inadequacy of funds to carry out minimally necessary supervision. It is a familiar story, retold after each scandal in the food and drug field, that the regulating agency in question was understaffed and could not keep up with the expansion of the industry and its products.

Remedial regulation as a governmental response to economic practices with undesirable spillover should be compared with the classic economic prescription for such situations to gain a true picture of the efficacy of regulation. In classic economic theory, spillover problems are dealt with by side-payments: the person causing the spillover effects is required to compensate everyone adversely affected until they are at least no worse off than they would be in the absence of his economic activity. Since such compensation is costly for the responsible individual he presumably will take steps to correct the offending practices, and some economic balance will be achieved. Specifically, he will reduce his spillover effects until the cost of further reduction equals the amount by which he could decrease his side-payments if he were to undertake further spillover reduction.

Two things should be noted about the classic economic solution. First, it does not guarantee that the offending activity will disappear, but only that its perpetrator will pay for the damage it causes. If this were the law, many companies might decide that it is cheaper to pay when they are caught than to change their practices.

Second, the pure economic solution is especially appropriate only when spillover effects fall on a few and can be readily calculated. When the lives of a large number of people are involved, as they are in the food and drug industries, direct payment becomes an inefficient and cumbersome way of adjusting the situation and the penalties that should be assessed are uncertain to begin with. For these reasons the political regulatory solution, with its attendant limitations, is often the more effective response to cases of undesirable spillover.

EXISTING, INTRINSICALLY UNDESIRABLE ACTIVITY

The fourth category comprises existing private economic practices that are intrinsically undesirable. Such practices are, or appear to be, to the immediate economic advantage of someone, since they do exist, but the social consensus is that they are undesirable regardless of their profitability to some. By definition, the practice in question cannot be redeemed by remedial regulatory action, but must be eradicated entirely. Thus the situation is one in which social goals override any consideration of the profits of the few because there is no possible compromise between the individual's freedom to carry out the given activity and society's freedom from the undesirable effects of such activity.

This category represents an extreme situation. Many economic practices that society would judge harmful escape regulation because their effects are slight or can easily be concealed from their victims and from regulatory agencies. Many other harmful economic activities are treated under category 3 by some form of regulation designed to mollify their bad effects while offering a minimum of interference to individuals for whom these activities are profitable. Very few socially harmful economic activities are obviously and uncontrollably detrimental and are thus marked for eradication.

Environmental pollution, a by-product of industrial operation, is a form of economic activity that both local and federal governments have often refused to accept. The larger and more visible the target, the more absolute has been the enforcement of pollution control. Individual homeowners in many parts of the country are still permitted to burn rubbish outdoors at specified hours of the day, although large companies have been frequent targets of local and national antipollution campaigns. Automobile manufacturers have been required to place antipollution devices on their products. Power companies have been particularly hard hit. Maximum limits on the sulphur content of coal used as fuel by power companies have been in effect in many states for some time, and the stringency of these standards in some states threatens to make the use of coal economically unfeasible in the near future.

Gambling is also viewed in most states as intrinsically undesirable, although federal regulation does not go much farther than registration and taxing by means of gambling stamps. In fact, where it is illegal, gambling provides a better example of the fourth type of regulation than pollution does. Pollution, a by-product of processes that generate desirable commercial goods, can often be eliminated without substantially altering the basic production process involved and it can therefore be treated as a category 3 situation. Subsidy techniques—tax writeoffs, for example—may even be useful in urging producers to clean up their operations, while in the pure category 4 situation, represented by gambling, strict suppression is the only effective policy device since the practices in question must be eliminated entirely.

NONEXISTING, DESIRABLE ACTIVITY

Roughly speaking, these are cases in which a potentially beneficial economic activity (public good) does not in fact exist, or exists in very short supply relative to the social need for it. Technically, in economics a public good is a commodity such as defense, whose consumption cannot effectively be denied to any person without denying it to all, and which otherwise can be enjoyed equally by all. Equity is an important consideration in the provision of public goods: since everyone benefits, everyone should pay. But in reality only those people who want a public good very much will be willing to pay for it, since all others will be assured of some free supply through the voluntary actions of others. For this reason public goods are usually inadequately supplied by voluntary market arrangements, and if their production costs are very large they probably will not be supplied at all. Government, with its superior ability to extract monetary support from the citizenry, is often the only agency capable of financing a pure public good.

One method of governmental finance is the user charge. Unfortunately, the user charge is not well adapted to the case of pure public goods. National defense is a good example since single individuals cannot forgo its benefits. In this situation the user charge is obviously superfluous because there are no nonusers, and easier ways can be devised for financing the activity.

Fire and police protection, considered broadly, also fall into this category. Although a limited form of fire fighting could perhaps be provided individually on a user charge basis, the costly installation of fire hydrants, the provision of fire prevention activities, fire inspection of public and commercial buildings, and so on usually dictate universal provision and some universal means of financing like taxes. Similarly, while limited property protection services are privately and individually available, most police activities—those viewed as prevention of crimes and accidents, preservation of public order, and the like—are obviously public goods that cannot easily be financed through user charges.

Other kinds of potentially desirable activities can be financed through user charges because different subscribers use differing amounts of the service, such as telephone and water utilities. The quasi-public good aspect of these utilities arises in that the capital costs necessary for them make local competition impractical, and also in that incomplete coverage of potential users by these utilities would substantially diminish their value to the remaining users. A telephone system would be limited in usefulness, for example, unless nearly everyone was connected to it. Similarly, the preservation of a steady supply of sanitary water would be much more difficult if many people tried to maintain private water and sewer systems.

How to provide desirable public goods has always been partly a matter of taste. From an interventionist viewpoint there are two choices: to preempt the activity for government completely, thus creating a public monopoly, or to allow a private monopoly to develop subject to specific governmental regulations.

It has been argued that some activities are national in scope and therefore require a national (governmental) monopoly. This argument has been made with regard to the mail system, for example. But recent experiments with private carriers in some cities show this argument to be incorrect. In fact, some of these experiments have suggested that there need not even be a local monopoly on mail delivery since private services have made a profit at lower rates competing directly against federal mail delivery.

In this connection it should be noted that the Johnson task force proposal for a private mail corporation, taken over by the Nixon administration, is not a move toward competition in mail handling, but is primarily a device to get around the political and management problems that the Post Office faces because it is a governmental agency. The choice between governmental operation and private (supervised) operation is thus being viewed as a choice of technique having certain implications for the mail system, but not as a crucial matter of policy.

Further evidence that the choice between government monopoly and private monopoly is not a crucial one comes from a comparison of mail service with telephone service. In the United States, mail service is a public monopoly and telephone service is a private regulated monopoly largely because of historical accident. Post offices and post roads were suggested early in our history as a continuation of English governmental practice. The telephone, on the other hand, was invented and developed privately and as a result has never become a public activity in the United States as it has in most other countries.

The appropriate governmental response to potentially desirable economic activity with large start-up costs has also been a problem in recent years because the number of such situations has increased and because the accounting in each situation is very complex. If the situation is truly one of a simple lack of private capital, then the appropriate governmental response is to provide a loan or other aid that will eventually be paid back at fair terms. Often however, the aid arrangement has been a hidden means of subsidy. In the case of the American supersonic transport, developed with government assistance until 1971, the terms of the agreement were such that the government probably would never have been fully repaid. It is quite possible that the airplane manufacturers, being reasonably sure that federal money could be obtained, overstated their financing and development difficulties in order to get federal aid.[3]

Governmental intervention can also be used to provide a desirable public good when the wish of some consumers not to purchase the good produces undesirable burdens for those who do. Old age and unemployment insurance are good examples. Regardless of the problem of private ability to pay for such insurance, some people with the necessary means will not provide for their own future and thus become a public burden to be supported by more foresighted individuals.

Perhaps the best remedy for this kind of problem would be to require all citizens to show evidence that their insurance needs are covered to some minimum level specified by law. The provision of such insurance could generally be through private insurance companies, with perhaps a supplementary minimum rate governmental program for citizens unable to afford any private program. This remedy is similar to that for automobile accident insurance, where coverage is provided through private firms but minimum insurance levels are set by state law.

A similar system could have been used nationally for unemployment compensation, but the economic circumstances of many workers during the Great Depression of the 1930s, when national unemployment compensation taxes went into effect, dictated quick action; a direct compulsory national program with rebates to existing state compulsory programs was chosen instead. Thus our compulsory social insurance arrangements, although responding to a genuine public need, have also been partly shaped by emergency circumstances. They may no longer be the most appropriate means of social insurance when government policy seems to be effective in preventing major economic emergencies.

Guidelines for public goods policy might be sought by looking simply to the question of private profitability: any supposed public good that cannot be supplied at a profit privately must be provided by governmental monopoly. But this criterion does not actually help very much. Even fire and police protection and national defense could be provided by a private producer at a profit, if he has the coercive power of the government to provide him with financing. There is no inherent difference in the nature of fire protection and electrical service that requires one to be a public monopoly and the other to be a regulated private monopoly.

For this reason a distinction on the basis of user charges provides better policy guidance. When an activity cannot be financed by user charges, and therefore cannot be undertaken for profit by private producers, governmental intervention takes place in response to overriding social goals. Regardless of the fact that national defense and fire and police protection would not be provided adequately by the economic market, for example, they are deemed sufficiently valuable that governmental action follows, either through imposition of a compulsory taxation financing arrangement or through actual governmental operation and ownership.

When an activity can be financed through user charges, however, it is more appropriate to speak of a conjunction between the goals of a potential private producer and the public's interest in having the benefit of valuable services. The tendency in user-charge services has been toward the regulated private monopoly. This is not an absolute relationship however: many American cities have acquired and maintained their own water, gas, or electric utilities, for example, generally operating them at a profit.

In short, no definite conclusion can be reached as to which policy course—private monopoly or public monopoly—is preferable. Large monopolistic enterprises are likely to have the common faults of bureaucracies whether they are public or private. One argument that may have some validity is that private monopolies, if they are not too strictly regulated (or subsidized) will be capable of responding to economic forces moving in the direction of greater competition, while public or heavily regulated monopolies will not be so flexible. Milton Friedman makes this argument in relation to the American transportation industry. He suggests that the ICC, established during the early period of American rail transportation when rail monopolies may have been necessary, has in fact protected existing railroads from competition that otherwise would have developed since the 1880s.[4] Even he, however, does not go so far as to say that public monopolies are always worse than private ones.

NONEXISTING, UNDESIRABLE ACTIVITY

For the purpose of offering policy guidelines, these two situations are largely hypothetical. It is logically impossible to speak of a governmental response in these situations because nothing has happened to which government can respond. To prevent undesirable activities from occurring, however, the appropriate governmental action is obviously some form of preventive regulation to outlaw such activities in advance. But most preventive regulation policies are not established until after some undesirable activity has already occurred, so in fact most policies of this type simply prevent the recurrence of undesirable activities.

State usury laws setting maximum interest rates on certain kinds of loans are an example of attempted preventive regulation. These laws were usually passed in response to political pressure from groups of aggrieved borrowers who felt that the interest rates they were paying were too high. Usury laws no longer attempt to curtail all interest-taking, but rather attempt to place a ceiling—usually about 8 percent—on the interest rates that lenders might otherwise be able to charge because of tight conditions in the money market.

Usury laws provide another illustration of the difficulties involved in regulatory policy when all that can be controlled are the symptoms of the problem. The money market is the real villain in this case, and it is not surprising that lenders have responded to market forces by inventing ways of bypassing interest rate ceilings, such as extra fee charges and padding of loan closing costs. Realization of the inevitability of tight money and high interest rates has contributed to the recent truth in lending laws, which do not attempt to prevent high interest charges but seek simply to require that the true interest charge be disclosed to the borrower. It is also symptomatic of the underlying problem that interest rate disclosure has not had any notable impact on the volume of consumer credit purchases.

Politics and Prescriptions

In conclusion, it should be emphasized again that individual political issues do not automatically fall into their proper places in the scheme outlined in this chapter. First, an analyst must answer the basic factual question of impact: how much effect does a given economic activity have, and on whom? Then he must make a value choice: whether, for example, an activity is sufficiently beneficial to warrant governmental attention, and if it is important enough, exactly what kind of governmental attention is called for. His own preferences will come into play here just as they would have in the ABM decision discussed earlier.

In the real world of politics, of course, competing analyses of political issues are the rule. Each party to a policy debate will supply his own interpretation of the facts to support his own position, and political decision makers will respond to some interpretations and reject others largely on the basis of their calculation of the political benefits and costs involved in each. As a result, actual policy decisions may not always appear to correspond to the "objective facts" of the issue at hand.

The final chapters of this book deal with three current policy questions from this point of view. Each of the three chapters develops the factual background of an issue, proposes a resolution for it, and finally examines the politics of the issue as a guide to the practicality of various proposed solutions. Each chapter provides only one interpretation of the issue it treats. The reader is encouraged to improve on the interpretation offered or construct his own analysis. Similarly, each chapter falls short of comprehensiveness in the data it presents, and the reader is encouraged to supplement this book with the many other sources available for each of the issues treated.

Notes

[1] Patent policies and their impact are described in *Government Patent Policy Study* (Boston: Harbridge House, 1968), a study commissioned by the Federal Council for Science and Technology.

[2] For a general discussion of these issues see Dale E. Hathaway, *Problems of Progress in the Agricultural Economy* (Chicago: Scott, Foresman, 1964).

[3] See J. A. Stockfisch and D. J. Edwards, "The Blending of Public and Private Enterprise: The SST as a Case in Point," *The Public Interest* No. 14 (Winter, 1969): 108–17.

[4] Milton A. Friedman, *Capitalism and Freedom* (Chicago: University of Chicago Press, 1962), pp. 28–29.

7

Wages, Prices, and Inflation

Inflation and Its Causes

Most of the economic theory surrounding the concept of price inflation is post-Keynesian, and in some ways it reflects the success of Keynesian economics. While Keynes assumed that the greatest danger in modern economies was inadequate demand, with its resultant depression and price deflation, American economic problems have often resulted from excessive stimulation of private economic expansion. On the whole it may be preferable to err on the side of excess in matters of economic growth, but to do so poses a real problem of persistent inflationary tendencies.

Broadly speaking, anti-inflationary policy is an example of category 3 (see chapter 6). No one wants to halt economic growth but nearly everyone professes a desire to correct its undesirable inflationary side effects. The political—and economic—problem comes in deciding whom to regulate and how. The major causes of post World War II inflation discovered by economic analysts are outlined below.[1] Appropriate policy depends on which of these causes is operating since they are each most responsive to a particular kind of policy measure. Anti-inflationary policy is further complicated by existing governmental stimulation of the economy —generally, category 5. The possibility should not be overlooked that government itself is the villain in some kinds of inflation.

DEMAND PULL INFLATION

If there is a "classic" mechanism for price inflation, it is that of demand pull, or "too many dollars chasing too few goods." This kind of inflation clearly reflects an overly successful Keynesianism, in that often the immediate cause of excessive total demand is governmental fiscal policy. The federal government may contribute to inflation by deficit spending during times of full employment, and it may also contribute indirectly to inflation through insufficiently restrictive tax policy or overly expansive monetary policy. The existence of continuous and substantial government involvement in economic management at the system level creates the opportunity for excessive governmental stimulation of the economy, either through direct federal spending or through encouragement of private consumer and business spending.

A substantial public (governmental) sector also contributes to the possibility of demand pull inflation because the government buys goods and services which do not satisfy direct consumer wants. During the Vietnam war buildup, for example, consumer demands did not change markedly and consumer purchasing power was held at high levels by the expansion of federal payrolls associated with the increased purchase of military hardware. An increased percentage of the GNP was preempted for foreign military purposes even though individual consumers did not revise their budgets or capital purchase plans to take account of these "common purposes" for which they were paying. Politically the average American may have supported the Vietnam war; economically he was reluctant to do so. The doctrine of sacrifice, of "guns or butter," was accepted by national decision makers but not by the American consumer.

Thus the short-run effect of Vietnam involvement was to siphon productive capacity from consumer goods to military hardware without substantially changing demand for consumer items, obviously resulting in increased demand for the consumer goods that were still available. Most public buying probably has a similar effect on the average consumer. Increased public expenditures for any purpose—police, national defense, farm subsidies, or whatever—subtract from the disposable income of consumers but do not displace other goods in consumer spending preferences. The inevitable result is demand pull inflation.

Economically the solution to demand pull inflation is simple; demand must be lowered through taxation or the market must be bypassed entirely through rationing of consumer goods or some similar device. Politically, of course, implementation involves real difficulties. Wars have provided the most common excuses for high tax levels and the only excuses for rationing acceptable in the United States; at other times presidents have encountered great difficulty in following fiscal policies appropriate to a state of demand pull inflation. A common argument among political cynics points out a tendency for politicians to spend but not to tax to pay for their extravagance. Congresses and presidents blame each other for this tendency; undoubtedly they are both partly guilty.

COST PUSH INFLATION

A second type of inflationary pressure builds up when economic competition is imperfect. In brief, the several kinds of cost push inflation result from the exercise of economic market power by private groups—either producers or groups of workers. A classic form of cost push inflation is produced by the seller who charges "all that the traffic will bear," meaning by implication that he is freed to some extent from normal competitive pressures and can therefore set his prices at will. The local miller in medieval times, for example, enjoyed this economic advantage over his customers, and his profits produced an artificial inflation in the price of bread and other products made from flour.

More recently, the nineteenth century business barons and twentieth century oligopolists and corporate monopolists have been accused of cost push inflation because they supposedly have used "market power" to extract maximum profit from the sale of their products at artificially high prices. The effect of these high prices may be passed directly to the consumer, or it may be passed indirectly through fabricators and other producers who in turn pass their high costs along to the consumer. This is the situation economists call "seller's inflation," which takes place through the mechanism of "administered prices" rather than through prices determined by the competitive market.

A second source of cost push inflation is the market power of industrial unions coupled with the market power of producers. Strong industrial unions are often accused of producing inflationary pressure in a given industry by demanding wage settlements in excess of the increase in their labor productivity since the previous wage agreement. Where an industry can administer its prices arbitrarily, unions are in a particularly favorable position because the increase in labor cost can simply be passed on to the consumer. Producers do not fight so hard when excessive labor union wage demands do not come out of profits. In fact, labor cost increases, especially where industry wide or "pattern" settlements apply, often become a kind of fixed expense which is automatically viewed as part of the cost of production to be charged to the buyer.

The impact of trade union power is similar. Typically, the trade union faces a labor market where there is one seller—the union—and a relatively large number of buyers—the producers. Since all producers face roughly the same labor costs and labor cost increases, these costs are again passed along to the consumer regardless of the inflationary consequences of the wage settlements in question.

In any case, the appropriate governmental response to cost push inflation is a direct regulatory one. Regulation may take several forms, depending on how the problem is defined. If large unions and oligopolies are viewed as either desirable or inevitable, then regulatory action must focus on a limitation of the pricing decisions made possible by union or producer market power. If unions and oligopolies are viewed as undesirable or unnecessary, then regulatory action can be directed at eliminating the market power which gives unions and oligopolies the ability to administer wages and prices in the first place.

STRUCTURAL INFLATION

Mention should also be made of structural inflation, which arises simply from the interdependence of the various sectors of the economy. In a competitive market economy, an independent shift of consumer demand—from automobiles to bicycles, for example—should produce a readjustment of prices, wages and employment levels in these two industries. But in the absence of perfect markets this readjustment need not occur. The successful resistance of unions and firms to any tendency toward lower wages or prices means that overall wages and price levels will always go up in response to any shift in the structure of demand. The increase in demand for household appliances at the expense of perishable food items, for example, will increase the price of appliances but it will not bring down the price of food because retailers and workers in the food industry will be able to resist market pressures to lower their wages and prices. Furthermore, price increases in appliances will eventually be passed along to the food industry and its employees as increased costs, so that upward pressure will ultimately be brought on food industry wages and prices also.

Inflational pressures resulting from structural demand changes can be lessened if fiscal policy is used to hold down aggregate demand, but this policy approach has a general effect on economic efficiency whose desirability must be weighed against the seriousness of inflationary pressures. For instance, if aggregate demand is lowered to the point where no industry generates inflationary wage or price decisions, overall economic growth will probably be much slower than that achievable at the level of demand corresponding to "full" employment. So price stability could be bought, but only at the price of inefficient, below-capacity production.

More serious is the possibility that the complete elimination of structural demand inflation would also mean the elimination of the normal allocation processes of the economy in response to changing demands. In the market economy (even with imperfections), raising wages and prices in a given sector is the natural way to attract labor and capital to that sector. This incentive for labor and capital mobility would be severely limited if it were never possible for any industry to offer inflationary wages or charge inflationary prices regardless of the state of their labor and goods markets. In fact, there need be no inconsistency between overall price stability and industry-to-industry variations in the rate of price change. Overall stability in the Consumer Price Index—the average price of a "market basket" of consumer goods and services—usually conceals some rapidly rising prices and some stable or falling prices, just as so-called full employment is only an average encompassing both job shortage and job surplus industries.

The real problem with structural inflation is not that prices increase in some sectors as demand shifts toward them, but that wages and prices do not come down proportionately in other sectors. From the economic point of view, then, the most appealing solution to structural inflation is some form of discretionary regulatory power that could be directed toward the sectors guilty of a failure to readjust to lower demand for their products. But what exactly do you tell such a regulatory agency? How does it decide how much inflation is permissible, or perhaps even necessary, for the health of a given industry? What industries should be singled out for special pressure to withhold price increases? Even leaving aside the political repercussions from the unequal application of regulatory pressure among the sectors of the economy, such positive regulation would also raise strong questions of workability and fairness.

In a limited sense, the federal government already has several selective regulatory devices, including the Federal Reserve Board's power over credit applicable to stock market transactions and its emergency powers over consumer and real estate credit in wartime, but these powers are not nearly specific or numerous enough to allow an effective attack on the many kinds of structural demand changes in the economy. These controls, including the investment tax credit, were devised for other purposes and are not adequate for price regulation of the kind demanded here.

PSYCHOLOGICAL INFLATION

The concepts of demand pull, cost push, and structural inflation all arise directly out of economic theory. But economists have long recognized that many economic phenomena can be explained completely only when market factors are supplemented by "irrational" peculiarities of individual consumer behavior, and the phenomenon of inflation is no exception. At times there seems to develop in the American public a set of attitudes which have loosely been called "inflationary psychology," in which price inflation, from whatever source, becomes accepted as an inevitable feature of economic life. In several ways an inflationary psychology produces inflationary pressures beyond those that would be expected from standard predictions of aggregate demand and production levels. First, consumers convinced of the inevitability of inflation are no longer deterred by rising prices. Their reaction when faced with price increases, to oversimplify a bit, is to draw on savings to make a desired purchase rather than wait until prices level off. By believing and acting as if prices never will level off, consumers strengthen immediate inflationary pressures through the creation of excessive aggregate demand. The panic buying at the beginning of the Korean war is an extreme example of this reaction.

Second, inflationary psychology puts unions under great pressure to keep their members "one step ahead" of inflation by making ever larger wage demands, even if these are known to be inflationary. A large wage settlement in one industry becomes an implicit challenge for unions in another industry, for though the first settlement was known to be inflationary the subsequent settlements must be even more inflationary if they are to represent any net gain over the rise of the cost of living. In the first nine months of 1969, for example, the average major union agreement represented a wage and fringe benefit boost of 8.1 percent, up from 6.6 percent in 1968 and 5.5 percent in 1967.[2]

A particularly subtle union response to inflationary psychology has also appeared recently in the timing of negotiated wage increases. Unions are coming to demand so-called "front-loaded" contracts, where most of the wage increase is packed into the first year of the contract in the hope that union members will be able to enjoy their higher income level before it is eaten up by inflation. Such wage demands provide an almost perfect example of a situation in which a group of individuals, each following an individual winning strategy, produces a situation in which everyone loses in the long run. But of course any individual union would be foolish to show wage restraint unless all unions did so at the same time, and in the absence of governmental regulation such restraint is unlikely to occur. Thus the understandable efforts of unions to win real gains for their members serve mainly to increase inflationary pressure at a time when such pressure is already great.

Third, inflationary psychology also contributes to aggregate demand increase through the mechanism of consumer credit. The truth-in-lending legislation passed in 1968 requiring retailers to disclose the annual percentage rate of their finance charges to credit customers has apparently had little effect on the volume of consumer credit, and consumer psychology provides an explanation for the law's lack of impact. When the cost of living increases by five percent a year, even the typical finance charges of eighteen percent a year begin to seem tolerable by comparison. In any case, if credit is available, there is no reason to wait to make a purchase, for the price will only be higher next year.

Inflationary psychology, by pushing consumers and labor unions into increased short-run spending and wage demands, produces an inflationary dynamic which is to some extent liberated from simple market-oriented expanations and therefore also somewhat resistant to market-oriented policy measures directed toward the reduction of aggregate demand. Presidents Johnson and Nixon unhappily discovered the truth of this proposition in the years after the rapid Vietnam buildup of 1965–66 and the deficit spending that financed that buildup. Economic growth and price inflation seemed to respond very sluggishly to a variety of strong policy measures including the combination of high bank interest rates ("tight money") and the ten percent income surtax enacted in 1968 and extended in 1969. Some commentators predicted the gloomy future of simultaneous recession and steady inflationary price creep, and by early 1970 their predictions had come true. Upward pressures on wages and prices did not respond to unemployment or slow economic growth because they were based in part on consumer feelings rather than rational calculations.

To the extent that inflation in the modern American economy is exacerbated by inflationary psychology, then, its solution obviously calls for direct governmental action against wage and price levels, of either the persuasive or the more stringent regulatory variety, as a supplement to the manipulation of aggregate demand. The simple application of aggregate fiscal and monetary techniques runs the risk of overdamping the economy and ending up with the worst of both worlds—a combination of unacceptable inflation and undesirable recession.

For the noneconomist, the relevance of the foregoing discussion of wage and price controls may have seemed questionable. But the basic point of the discussion is simple: the phenomenon consumers experience as inflation—shrinkage of the effective purchasing power of their paychecks—may result in reality from a variety of causes. The mix of inflationary causes demands a mix of policy responses, otherwise policy makers risk merely treating symptoms or penalizing one segment of the economy for faults that are more widespread and for which responsibility should be more widely shared.

The Guidepost Experience

LESSONS OF THE FIFTIES

Before considering the possible uses of wage and price controls more specifically, it may be instructive to look at the history of federal wage-price guideposts, the major fund of peacetime experience from which some conclusions can be drawn about the feasibility of more stringent controls.

In some ways the concern of Kennedy's Council of Economic

Advisers for the inflation problem grew out of the persistence of price inflation during the otherwise peaceful and economically stable decade following the conclusion of the Korean war. For at least twenty years prior to 1953 the economy could not have been considered stable for long enough to allow any firm conclusions about its "normal" performance to be drawn. Either depression conditions, active wartime mobilization or postwar readjustment and demobilization obscured the underlying pattern of economic performance during the presidencies of Franklin Roosevelt and Truman, preoccupying the attention of economic policy makers with economic fluctuations rather than economic regularities.

Thus the eight Eisenhower years provided the first sustained view of Cold War economic normality. Balancing the normal economy in this period required enough ingenuity that the activist advisers who came to power under President Kennedy began to look around for more effective and flexible tools to assist the president in carrying out his statutory responsibility for stable economic growth. Several of the existing tools have been mentioned briefly in chapter 5.

Wage and price guideposts seem to have developed quite naturally from the identification by Kennedy's economic advisers of supposedly irresponsible actions on the part of industrial firms and large industrial unions. Price increases in basic industries generally went unchallenged during Eisenhower's term because of the moderate, hands-off stance advocated by Eisenhower's advisers Arthur F. Burns and Raymond J. Saulnier and the influence of Eisenhower's economically conservative Treasury Secretary, George Humphrey. These advisers viewed their job primarily as the exercise of fiscal responsibility in government, the pursuit of the balanced budget, and the careful use of monetary policy to smooth out business cycles. The relatively high unemployment and unused productive capacity levels during the 1950s held down inflationary pressures even though price increases in some basic industries were widely supposed to be inflationary. An influential study conducted in 1959 under the sponsorship of the Joint Economic Committee, for example, concluded that steel price rises directly and indirectly accounted for forty percent of the increase in consumer prices between 1947 and 1958.[3]

The power of organized labor was also a matter of public concern during the 1950s. In 1955 the American Federation of Labor and the Congress of Industrial Organizations finally united as the AFL-CIO, lending popular credence to supposed union power. Union corruption was the subject of several sets of congressional investigations and prompted the Labor Management Reporting and Disclosure Act of 1959 (the Landrum-Griffin Act). Several long strikes in basic industries, including a 1959 steel strike that lasted over 100 days, revived public fears of the excessive power of large unions. Nevertheless, President Eisenhower did not take especially strong stands against union wage demands. He was more willing to use the injunction procedures of the Taft-Hartley act than President Truman had been, but invocation of Taft-Hartley did not always guarantee that a strike would be settled or that the strike settlement, when reached, would be noninflationary.

In this domestic setting it is not surprising that Kennedy and his Council of Economic Advisers turned to direct action against wage and price increases. But Kennedy's view encompassed more than just the American economy. His interest in world politics led also to an interest in international economics and the U.S. balance of payments. Lowering of trade barriers was one of his policy goals; so also was improvement of the trade position of U.S. exports. The 1962 report of the Council of Economic Advisers, introducing the wage-price guideposts, justified a pricing policy largely with reference to the foreign trade position of U.S. industry and the resulting balance of payments between the United States and the rest of the world. For Kennedy then, domestic price stability was part of a larger picture of long range U.S. economic prosperity in a world context.

Finally, wage-price guideposts, dependent on moral suasion for their success, fit well with Kennedy's concept of his office. Kennedy thought that the presidency should be a kind of energizer that provides the motive force for governmental and private action conducive to broad national goals. In attempting to move others, the president's primary resource was his persuasive ability—his ability to set goals and to focus public attention on them. In the "energizer presidency," persuasion bridged the gap between presidential responsibilities (always expanding) and presidential powers (chronically inadequate). Persuasion is especially important in the private economic sphere, where presidents have enjoyed little direct power except in war and depression emergencies. Thus wage and price guideposts were best suited to the Kennedy leadership style and at the same time the strongest weapon appropriate for a free-enterprise economy.

THE GUIDEPOST RATIONALE

During their short career between 1962 and 1969, the wage-price guideposts were consistently stated and defended in the annual reports of the Council of Economic Advisers. The statements were as follows:

> The general guide for noninflationary wage behavior is that the rate of increase in wage rates (including fringe benefits) in each industry be equal to the trend rate of over-all productivity increase. General acceptance of this guide would maintain stability of labor cost per unit of output for the economy as a whole—though not of course for individual industries.
>
> The general guide for noninflationary price behavior calls for price reduction if the industry's rate of productivity increase exceeds the over-all rate—for this would mean declining unit labor costs; it calls for an appropriate increase in price if the opposite relationship prevails; and it calls for stable prices if the two rates of productivity increase are equal.[4]

Exceptions to these general guides were specifically made for very low wage workers, for shifts into shortage occupations, for shifts out of industries of chronic underemployment, and for particularly profitable or particularly unprofitable businesses.

Although the guideposts were stated in general terms which

could be applied to any industry, their intended targets were much more specific. In their annual reports the Council always stated that the political-economic rationale for the guideposts was their contribution to responsible behavior on the part of unions and industries with substantial market power. Competitive industries and labor markets supposedly would fall into line through the operation of normal market pressures. The wage and price guidelines may have been more confusing and threatening than they were intended to be, since theoretically they envisioned sweeping price cuts but actually they were invoked only against excessive price increases, and then only in a few key industries.

The guideposts were first specifically enunciated in the 1962 report of the Council of Economic Advisers, although in their emphasis on the need for private economic responsibility they followed a line of argument extending back at least as far as the Council's 1957 report. The Council moved very cautiously toward specific suggestions, at first billing the guideposts merely as a "contribution to public discussion" of responsible wage-price actions. In 1962 the Council also hesitated to provide a single productivity figure, choosing instead to present a number of curves of output per man hour over the previous ten years. For any interested observer, inspection of the curves would of course yield a productivity guide, in this case ranging between 2.9 percent per year and 3.7 percent per year, depending on which curve was chosen from the chart.

In the 1963 Council report the general guidelines were repeated but no productivity figures or graphs appeared in the text to make the guidelines more specific. In 1964 and 1965 specific figures of 3.2 percent per year appeared in the discussions of wage and price guideposts, but only obliquely (as five-year trend averages in a table). The 1966 report contained an extensive discussion of the guideposts and some of their supposed successes in steel and aluminum, and it admitted that the Council had been using a 3.2 percent productivity guide. The 1966 report concluded with an expression of concern that private decisions would undermine the guideposts and it threatened restrictive fiscal and monetary measures if private actions should precipitate a wage-price spiral.

The 1967 report of the Council of Economic Advisers contained a brief history of the wage-price guideposts and a description of the persuasive and educational activities carried on by the Council and other governmental officials on behalf of the guidepost policy. It reported, for example, that the Council became involved in price increase cases concerning fifty product lines during 1966, some by invitation of the producers but most by Council initiation. The report cited the cost of living increase of more than 3 percent during 1966 and conceded that wage settlements would not remain within the guideposts for that reason, but it also reiterated the long run validity of the productivity guideposts for wages. The Council advocated producer absorption of cost increases, including wage settlements, citing rapid expansion of profits during 1966 as justification for price restraint. The same expectations and policies were repeated in 1968.

The 1969 Council report conceded implicitly that the guidepost notions had lost their usefulness. It argued that the "wage-price upturn" of 1965–68 was due to excess demand generally and to early price increases in farm products, raw materials, and services, all areas where, the Council admitted, guideposts have little application. The Council offered no specific wage-price policy for 1969, certainly in large part because of the imminent changeover of administrations, but also because nothing new could be said in the context of the guidepost notions. The 1969 chapter on price stability concluded with a call for cooperation between labor and business in formulating new guideposts to which both sides could adhere voluntarily.

DID THE GUIDEPOSTS WORK?

An evaluation of the economic impact of the wage-price guideposts is a difficult task. From the perspective of 1967, Walter Heller, Chairman of the Council of Economic Advisers which invented them, was unwilling to grant the guideposts any specific degree of economic success in 1961–65 even though wages and prices did in fact move within the guideposted limits.[5]

Skeptics would say that voluntary guideposts work as long as it is comfortable for business and labor to go along with them—during times of low inflationary pressure—and that voluntarism breaks down when it is most needed—in times of inflationary tendencies in the economy. Certainly a surface analysis of wage-price guideposts supports this conclusion, for their apparent success in 1962–65 came during a period of return toward full employment. The 1966–68 period, when the guideposts failed, was a period of economic "overactivity" generated by Vietnam spending and other causes.

But this argument ignores the possibility that business and labor can be independent causes of inflationary pressure, or at least discretionary transmitters of such pressure to the average consumer, and it is against this kind of discretionary power that the guideposts were consistently applied. It could even be argued (but not readily tested) that the existence of specific guideposts moderated inflationary wage and price settlements even when such decisions were substantially above the guideposts. Arthur M. Okun, one of Johnson's CEA chairmen, claims that "jawboning" did have this effect.[6]

A disturbing counterargument that has been advanced implies that the guideposts in part simply deferred inflationary pressures resulting from discretionary market power. The absence of price decreases in industries with rapidly rising productivity in the early 1960s resulted in large profits that justified large wage demands, especially when labor unions began to feel the pinch of price inflation in the later 1960s. At that time the Council suggested that business absorb cost increases into the high profit levels prevailing, but this second-best remedy could not prevent excessive wage increases. Okun partly acknowledges this argument by pointing to the rapid price rises in jawboned industries after 1969, when the Nixon administration set the jawbone aside.[7]

The resistance of wages and prices to downward adjustment is a problem beyond the scope of guideposts, one ingrained in the notion of market power on the part of unions and producers, and it does seem to set an outside limit on the success of guideposts even under the most favorable conditions. The Council was not unaware of this problem either, but all they could suggest was that direct market power controls, such as anti-merger policies, would be valuable companions to the guideposts.

Finally, the reader should not suppose that the wage and price successes enjoyed by Presidents Kennedy and Johnson resulted entirely from voluntary guidepost adherence. On many occasions the "education" involved in "laying on" of the guideposts was supplemented by the market power of the federal government itself, the battle for price stability thus becoming a simple power clash between big government and big business.

In aluminum and copper, for instance, Johnson administration threats to dump government stockpiles of these metals on the market were apparently effective in forcing reconsideration of proposed price increases. President Kennedy in 1962 rather pointedly had Defense Secretary Robert McNamara announce that if price rises went through as scheduled, the administration would have to reconsider pending steel purchase contracts, throwing new purchases to companies that chose not to increase their prices. In 1967 a threatened cut in tariff barriers and an increase in import quotas on oil and gas were used against price rises in this industry.

In each of these instances governmental economic power was a potent force, either because of the sheer size of federal economic activity or because of the substantial impact of federal import policy on the domestic economy. The resort to such powers suggests something of the presidential frustration with persuasion and guideposts, and also reveals how critical price stability was in their overall economic policies. For Kennedy and Johnson, at least, voluntary controls were not strong enough.

The Economics of Controls

It is easy to suppose that a given policy, economic or otherwise, is failing because it lacks "teeth." In wage and price restraint, many commentators have said, in effect, "if they won't do it voluntarily, we'll make them do it." The student of public policy should always ask himself two questions when he encounters this kind of statement: "Can we do it politically?" and, "Even if we can do it, will it work?" Answers to these questions are complicated, but both questions should be asked to guard against the risk of leaping at the first "obvious" solution that presents itself.

A free enterprise economy is an elaborate mechanism, and it is always a good bet that a solution for one sector's problems will be ineffective, or worse, in another sector. Such is the case for wage and price controls.

To add some element of realism to a discussion that must necessarily be brief, oversimplified, and somewhat abstract, we can analyze a simplified economy having only seven sectors, aside from government. Each sector is in a slightly different economic situation and will therefore view the question of wage and price controls in a slightly different way from the others.

The sectors are:

1. Services and professionals,
2. Retailers and other small businesses,
3. Small manufacturers,
4. Extractive and basic manufacturing industries,
5. New technological "clean" industries,
6. Organized labor unions, and
7. Consumers.

Controls can be imposed on the first six of these sectors; the seventh is supposedly the beneficiary of controls applied to the others.

THE SERVICE SECTOR

For group 1, services and professionals, prices are virtually the same as wages since the workers are independent operators or gain a large proportion of their income from tips rather than wages paid by their employers. For this analysis, then, services can be defined as products of which labor is the major proportion of the cost.

In applying wage-price controls to this group, or in considering their application, it should first of all be obvious that price regulation is nearly equivalent to wage regulation. Thus simultaneous direct controls over wages and prices would never be needed here. A second important fact about the services and professionals (who also perform services) is that wages are not set in a competitive market but are usually set with reference to some external standard.

For many services involving low levels of skill, a statutory minimum wage is the relevant wage standard and therefore the productivity assumptions applied by wage-price guideposts have little application. Hotel porters and restaurant waiters, for example, have probably not increased their labor productivity commensurate with the increase in the standard expected tip. Instead, their base wages and standard tips are set in some relationship to a minimum living standard and in that sense are paid for, as they must be, out of general productivity increases in other industries.

Other service occupations have become unionized and have thereby escaped both the rigors of market competition and the applicability of statutory minimum wages. For barbers, for example, labor productivity has not changed appreciably in recent years, and fee setting by the barbers' union is done in relation primarily to the cost of living and to the rise in general affluence of barbershop customers.

In both unionized and nonunionized service occupations, our unstated policy is that some socially essential occupations must receive adequate compensation even if that means going far beyond the standard of market value or labor productivity. In the short run the minimum wage could be held down by governmental action or the monopoly power of unions could be broken by legal action, and these measures would eliminate inflationary pressure from the service industry, but eventually wage levels and price levels would have to move upward again if any supply at all of these services was to be provided. Thus the best that can be hoped for in applying an anti-inflationary policy to the service occupations is that their price levels will not increase any faster than average productivity (the standard under the former wage-price guideposts) and that "catch-up" increases in the statutory minimum wage will be relatively small in economic impact and therefore easily absorbed by the economy as a whole.

Much the same situation prevails for professional services such as medical and dental care. Most doctors and dentists are self-employed, and their fees are set in relation to internal professional standards and to the cost of living generally. Obviously, wage and price controls in this area do not fit economic realities very well, and their arbitrary application would understandably raise a storm of complaint. The informal procedures by which fees are set render any formalized approach such as mediation or case-by-case regulation either irrelevant or impracticable.

RETAIL TRADE

Group 2, retailers, can also quickly be dismissed as an inappropriate target for wage and price controls. Retailers add no value to the products they sell other than those associated with the convenience of local shopping for consumers. Retailers generally attain lower selling prices by maintaining high rates of turnover relative to inventory, physical facilities, and other fixed costs, and most of them operate on small profit margins with a high proportion of costs that are beyond their immediate control. Thus the proper target of anti-inflationary action here must be the supplier or the manufacturer, and not the retailer, whose independent impact on prices is minimal.

Of course labor costs do figure highly in many retailing operations, but generally wages are paid either to the owner and his relatives (in the "mom and pop" store, which is specifically exempted from minimum wage coverage) or to nonunion labor where statutory minimum wages apply. In either case wage levels are not set in relationship to productivity, and productivity is nearly impossible to measure. In comparison with the general run of wages in American industry, the wages paid to retail sales employees are low enough to fall under the low-wage exception to wage-price guideposts, and probably should also be so treated under any scheme of wage-price controls. This conclusion is reinforced by the fact that only a small fraction of the retail price of most consumer goods is cost added by the retail merchant. The bulk of the cost to the consumer is added through raw materials, fabricating, and handling, and it is in these areas that wage and price controls would more logically be applied.

SMALL MANUFACTURERS

The situation for small manufacturing concerns is similar in some ways to retailing and in others to large-scale manufacturing enterprise. The similarity to small retailing enterprise is the small manufacturer's general lack of market power. At best the market for small manufactures is competitive; at worst it forces them to sell into a market where the buyer (a larger manufacturer) has market power and can enforce lower selling prices if he wishes.

If the small manufacturer sells in a competitive market there is little cause for direct concern about his prices because any tendency toward charging excessive prices will be checked by competition within the market in classic economic fashion. This is the ideal situation, which governmental regulation seeks to reestablish; if it already exists there is no cause for positive governmental intervention.

If the small manufacturer sells to buyers who can partially control his selling price then concern may properly be directed at the behavior of the buyer. Presumably such market power would be used to hold down selling prices; therefore governmental intervention would have to be justified on grounds of preservation of competition rather than on grounds of inflationary price settlements that might be reached in the absence of regulation.

On the labor side, small manufacturing is much less similar to small retail enterprise. Small manufacturers usually have a unionized work force, which in principle is capable of demanding inflationary wage settlements. But such power is not by itself cause for concern because it does not necessarily imply that unions can make inflationary demands stick. If the unions in the industry are decentralized so that their demands are met by each firm in relation to the competitive and profit situation of that firm, then there is little cause for alarm because managers will be economically unable to settle for wage increases that outrun labor productivity by very much. If they were to do so in the short run they (and the company's stockholders) would eventually have to pay through decreased sales (sales loss to competitors) and lower profits.

A more common situation today is for unions to bargain on an industrywide basis for identical wage scales for all the firms in an industry, or for contract settlements achieved with large firms (and sometimes even firms outside the industry) to serve as patterns for settlement with smaller members of the industry. In either of these situations the individual producer in the industry is in no position to fight the industrywide trend, nor does he have any incentive to do so. Labor settlements that are uniform across an industry become simply the equivalent of additional fixed costs for all members of the industry, to be passed along to the consumer in similar price increases by all firms. The relative competitive positions of the member firms have not changed, and normal competitive processes can resume at the higher price level once a period of adjustment has occurred. For industries where competition is strong and union demands are a substantial part of costs, the best anti-inflation policy is therefore one aimed at union power, since firms in the industry merely transmit cost changes to the public. Where this is the case, direct action against prices is unnecessary.

THE BASIC INDUSTRIES SECTOR

This group, encompassing the "old" basic and extractive industries, includes many of the classic oligopolies and monopolies in the American economy. Unions in these industries are strong and are organized industrywide, and firms have some measure of product market power which enables them to administer their prices within at least a limited range. Wage-price control here is properly concerned with the interplay of union power and company power. Unions in these industries usually have enough economic resources to make inflationary wage demands, but at the same time companies have potential countervailing economic power they may call into play if a contract dispute threatens to become a strike.

In fact strikes are often an expected way of labor-management relations in these industries, where the heritage of antiunion violence in the 1930s, when the major industrial unions were being formed, is still invoked by labor leaders as a rallying point. The likelihood of a strike is known well in advance and production generally speeds up before the expiration of a contract to provide a backlog to fill orders anticipated during the strike period. Purchasers also accelerate their orders to be certain of obtaining a supply even if a strike does occur. For their part unions collect extra dues from their members to build up a sizable strike fund, thus expressing a credible determination to strike for a long period if necessary and at the same time making provisions for the economic welfare of their workers during the strike.

The existence of massive economic resources on the part of labor and management does not guarantee anything about the form of wage and price decisions to come out of a new contract. Most specifically, a company may choose not to engage in periodic and costly strikes if it knows that it will probably give in anyway after a token resistance and a few days or weeks of strike-disrupted production. The availability of control over prices makes this "easy out" both possible and appealing, and it seems to be taken quite often in basic industries like steel and automobiles. Since wage settlements in these industries are generally industrywide, either because unions are industrywide or because pattern contract settlements are made for the industry as a whole, there is an added temptation also to accept large union demands after an appropriate show of resistance has been made for the benefit of the public and the stockholders.

Given their economic situation, both labor and management act in a perfectly rational manner by following the procedures just outlined. The only difficulty is that these perfectly logical actions may have important undesirable consequences for the public at large, and it is these inflationary consequences that give rise to the possibility of governmental intervention. But even here, where market power is obviously in evidence, wage and price controls are not the only economically workable solutions. It would be perfectly possible, for example, to apply antitrust regulation to both labor and management in a "trust-busting" effort to break up the market power that gives them both the ability to administer prices and wages.

As far as the public impact is concerned, an equivalent and more common proposal would involve applying antitrust controls to industry alone, thus pushing large manufacturers back into the competitive situation of smaller manufacturers. But in view of the industrywide labor settlements in large manufacturing, even trust-busted industries would not compete over wage cost increases, and the public would still feel inflationary pressure from high wage demands.

Aside from the economic difficulties in one-sided regulation, there are objections that manufacturers would make on grounds of simple fairness. To force them back into a competitive situation by governmental action without treating the oligopolistic or monopolistic labor union control of industrial workers, all in the name of price stability, would place the entire burden of intervention on the management side. Complaints would be understandably bitter if the responsibility for inflation were placed solely on business since, in reality, management and labor share that blame in roughly equal parts.

Antitrust action is, on the whole, an unwieldy device for wage and price control. By its nature such action aims for permanent long-range effects, and the complex litigation that surrounds major antitrust cases invariably lengthens their implementation time even more. In markets where productive processes exhibit economies of scale, it can also be argued that trust busting would actually raise prices by inducing inefficiency. A case can be made for an anti-merger policy that would prevent mergers unless they led to greater production efficiency, but such a policy would not be very effective against price inflation because it would not check existing market power.

If antitrust action were eliminated on grounds of equity, or because it represents a somewhat ineffective long-range attack on a short-range problem, several solutions are left for the basic industries. Each involves the use of direct controls. Here, as in antitrust, one-sided measures are unfair and offer no guarantee of results. Arbitrary limitation of price increases, for instance, without a ceiling on labor wage demands, would force manufacturers to do all the adjusting themselves under labor-management conditions that would not necessarily lead to an economically stable industry. Profits can be squeezed only so far, even in a monopoly, before investment and development (to say nothing of stockholders and stock prices) begin to suffer. Also, while such a one-sided solution could be favored as being the minimal governmental intervention necessary to do the job, it violates normal standards of regulatory fairness by restricting one side and not the other.

Application of wage controls alone, on the other hand, would not necessarily do the job of stopping inflationary price increases because manufacturers would still have market power to administer prices and they might choose to do so even in the absence of labor demand excuses. The steel industry, for example, has claimed modernization expenses as a justification for higher prices and higher profits in the past, and such exceptions were allowed in the wage-price guideposts operating during the 1960s. At best, governmental supervision of these price increases would be needed, and an extensive bureaucracy would undoubtedly develop to determine whether a given price increase was justified. For these basic industries, then, a combination of wage and price controls is called for when both the economic and equity arguments are considered.

TECHNOLOGICAL INDUSTRY

For the newer technologically oriented industries (those specializing in military and defense construction and electronics) the notion of governmental intervention seems almost inappropriate because many of these firms have a close and continuing relationship with government through contracts and implicit or explicit market guarantees. According to John Kenneth Galbraith, some of the basic economic assumptions about the operation of big business need to be changed to correspond to developments in the modern American economy, especially as they relate to the newer industries. In *The New Industrial State* he argues that these industries can be characterized by a decline in the importance of unionized labor relative to a "technostructure" favorably oriented toward the corporation, and the gradual replacement of profit maximization as a management goal with a management policy designed to maximize stable growth of the corporation through steady investment.[8]

In addition, many of the technologically oriented industrial firms operate at least partly on the basis of "demand by contract" where, the evidence indicates, there is little pressure toward holding down wages and prices. To begin with, most contracts for new defense hardware are let on the basis of development expertise rather than on the state of existing products sold by the company acting as supplier. Usually during the course of a contract the contracting agency changes specifications for the product, with the result that contractors can easily allow product cost to rise without apparent limit. The C5A cargo plane, for example, was contracted for in 1965 at a rate of 120 planes for $3.1 billion, but by 1968 the Air Force estimated the cost for 120 planes at $4.3 billion.

Similarly, most contracts are sold as lump items rather than as a series of component parts. Separation of a project into more manageable pieces takes place through private subcontracting, and often when the entire package is reassembled the prime contractors have added a percentage profit figure for themselves onto the amount due the subcontractors. In lump sum contracting the contracting governmental agencies do not know in detail what component parts of the contract are involved or how they are being paid. Further, since large hardware items are extremely specialized, competition is frequently lacking. In the eight fiscal years ending June 30, 1969, only 13 percent of Department of Defense procurement was effected through competitive bidding, 31 percent through competitive negotiation, and the remaining 56 percent through "single source" negotiation. Of the fiscal 1969 procurement total of $40.7 billion, only 11 percent involved competitive bids.[9]

The candid attempts of government agencies in recent years to channel business to contract-dependent firms who have lost out on a series of recent contracts (aid to the faltering Lockheed Corporation, for example) again indicates that there is little effort made in the "demand by contract" sector to bolster the kinds of "natural" economic controls on wage and price levels that would ordinarily operate.

Price inflation obviously may occur in this sector owing simply to the difficulty of measuring unit costs and prices and also to the ease of obscuring actual costs so as to draw larger profits than would otherwise be the case. Considering the technical difficulties in applying wage and price controls to this industry, however, and also the elaborate interconnections already existing between government agencies and industries in this sector, it quickly becomes apparent that the present methods of contract control and oversight, coupled with occasional congressional hearings about cost overruns and other contract scandals, are more appropriate to this sector than are direct controls.

Galbraithian arguments, by pointing away from the simple labor-management conflict model to one involving a large degree of cooperation, reinforce the conclusion that special wage and price controls are probably not appropriate here. The significance of unions is low and declining in these technological industries, meaning either that union wage demands need not be accepted or that they are such a small percentage of total cost that their impact on price is minor. Second, if the firm works on the assumption of stable growth rather than profit maximization it will often be willing to absorb excessive labor demands or extraordinarily high (and undeserved) salary rates for technical personnel rather than risk a work stoppage or inability to compete for a new contract. Thus the new technological firm, even when it is faced with inflationary cost pressures as great or greater than those in other

Table 6
Ideal Anti-inflation Policy, by Sector

Sector	*Preferred technique*
Services and professionals	None applicable
Retail trade	None directly applicable; focus instead on supplier prices
Small manufacturers	Union trust busting
Basic manufacturers	Business and labor trust busting, labor-management mediation
Technological industries	Government contract supervision and oversight

sectors, may be less likely to pass these costs along directly to the public in the manner of the old-time retailer.

WAGE AND PRICE ECONOMICS: A SUMMARY

The analysis here, even in its greatly simplified form, has demonstrated the proposition that the appropriateness of controls depends a lot on the sector in question. Some sectors appear almost entirely free from blame while others are definitely culpable. Even for the culpable, however, direct wage and price controls may not be the most appropriate regulatory device. Table 6 summarizes the discussion of this chapter as far as the most appropriate kind of wage and price regulation is concerned; next to be answered is the separate question of whether it is feasible in the American political process to impose wage or price controls on anyone at all.

The Political Feasibility of Controls

JAWBONING AND THE NIXON ADMINISTRATION

For the American economy, wage and price controls have usually been viewed as desperate measures for desperate situations. When they have been used, their justification has always had an emergency character and, with few exceptions, controls have been terminated as soon as return to the free market was at all feasible.

Only voluntary measures such as the wage-price guideposts in effect during the Kennedy and Johnson administrations have received substantial support as routine executive economic powers.

In the past decade, however, the stubborn persistence of price inflation, despite fluctuations in employment and economic growth rates, has pushed wage-price controls higher on the list of yet-to-be-tried solutions to the nation's economic problems. In 1969 and 1970, especially, pessimism about the seeming immunity of simultaneous inflation and recession to strict economic measures produced a spectacular decline in the stock market and a crescendo of plaintive cries for action from all quarters.

Even a moon landing and a stream of optimistic Presidential pronouncements on the state of the economy did not free President Nixon, and he found it necessary to appear on nationwide radio and television more than once to defend his economic policies. He also committed his administration to a mild form of the "jawboning" policies that he had earlier argued against, by appointing a productivity commission and directing the CEA to announce periodic "inflation alerts" to focus public attention on inflationary pressures generated by specific industries.

In the thick of the battle in 1970 President Nixon found an impressive group arrayed against him, including two former CEA chairmen, major Democratic party spokesmen, the chairman of the Federal Reserve Board, George Meany of the AFL-CIO, influential business figures including the American Bankers Association, and at least one member of his own cabinet. Against this opposition, especially that of his former close adviser, Fed chairman Arthur Burns, President Nixon's action was remarkably restrained and presumably reflected his determination to follow a hands-off policy even in the face of a near-emergency situation.

Scheduled contract expirations in 1970, including several in large basic industries, made Nixon's position even more significant as a statement of policy. The United Auto Workers and the automobile manufacturers were already girding for a showdown, and Nixon's statement could have been interpreted as an implicit go-ahead for inflationary settlements in this and other industries.

Early in 1971 President Nixon dealt with a similar problem

in the construction trades, and in that case he also acted with great restraint. Following several weeks of speculation, trial balloons, and vague threats of strong governmental action, the administration took the relatively minor step of suspending provisions of the Davis-Bacon Act which require contractors on federal construction projects to pay prevailing wage rates. Within a short time the Davis-Bacon provisions were reinstated and a consultative mechanism was set up to allow a measure of governmental pressure on wage negotiations in the construction industry. Reportedly President Nixon overruled several of his advisers when they suggested imposing wage and price controls on the industry.[10]

In reality it is probably impossible for any modern President to refrain completely from interference in the economy, and some of Nixon's adamant rejection of the "moral suasion" involved in jawboning may have been primarily for business consumption. At least his refusal to jawbone did not prevent his use of other means of presidential pressure. In January of 1970, for instance, he ordered a study of the pricing policies and market conditions in the copper industry, articulating a previously unannounced administration policy to "watch markets that may be out of line" and that therefore might have an adverse economic effect. To underline governmental interest in the copper industry President Nixon appointed study commission members from his Council of Economic Advisers, the Commerce Department, the Interior Department, the State Department and the Office of Emergency Preparedness. Other industries, especially those selling large amounts to the federal government, undoubtedly noted this action by the Nixon administration and at least had to give some credence to the possibility of subtle administration pressure on prices, whether publicly announced or not.

CONTROLS AND THE PUBLIC

At first glance it may seem strange that no public outcry is raised against the kind of arbitrary interference the federal government practices in copper, steel, and other basic goods. Americans, after all, are brought up to believe in notions of laissez faire, free enterprise, and minimal governmental interference as the ideals on which the country is based. Certainly just the thought of a President trying to push around a businessman is sufficient cause for protest. That a President should also claim a right to interfere as a responsibility and prerogative of his office is nearly unthinkable.

Generally this characterization *is* still true, but for several reasons it has not been a powerful political factor in the last few years. In the first place, most of the recent Presidential actions against excessive inflationary wages and prices have been those of Democratic presidents, and these have been primarily against big business rather than against big labor. A relatively small number of people identify themselves as business sympathizers when the issue is posed as "business against the public" as it was during the Kennedy and Johnson presidencies. Indeed, issues pitting the power of big business against the public, like pollution and prices, have mobilized more public protest in the last few years than have issues like wages and featherbedding that pit big business against the interests of organized labor. One possible reason for this phenomenon is the increasing tendency for the average American to believe in a conspiracy of the "bigs"—big business and big government—against him and his interests. But whatever the reasons, the American "business society" has apparently produced enough people antipathetic to business interests that governmental regulation is no longer as terrifying in reality as it used to be in theory.

Social researchers have also noted a strain of vindictiveness running through the average American's concept of justice—a sense that justice is primarily retribution for misdeeds committed. Somewhat the same feeling attends the imposition of informal pressure on businesses to lower prices, as evidenced during the period of more-or-less successful wage and price guideposts. If the President took action against a supposedly errant company, this action fell within the range of acceptable retribution for the excessive profits everyone "knew" the company was making.

There is little direct evidence for the speculations just offered but there is substantial evidence that Americans, if the conditions are right, will accept wage and price controls with relatively little resistance. Our willingness to accept controls is related to the apparent seriousness of the economic situation as it is communicated to the general public through news releases, Presidential pronouncements and other official statements. Of course, the questions that are posed to the average American in determining his willingness to use wage and price controls always frame the problem in an emergency context—moreover, they are always asked during an emergency—and therefore they give little indication of what the person responding would prefer to do if the situation were not so clearly out of control.

Nevertheless, the figures in public opinion polls are quite convincing in themselves. They show a remarkable public willingness to freeze wages and prices, obviously reflecting deep public unhappiness about price inflation and also the public's tendency to blame inflation on someone else. In June 1970, for example, a Gallup poll showed that 48 percent of those interviewed favored a wage-price freeze. This figure compares closely with the 55 percent approval rating for wage-price controls in the serious buying rush shortly after the beginning of the Korean war, and it is a comment on the public's judgment of the magnitude of inflation in 1970.

Shortly after the Gallup poll in June 1970, a study conducted by the normally reliable Minnesota Poll showed that 73 percent of Minnesota residents interviewed felt that wage-price controls were needed. Of course some groups in the public favor these controls more than others do. Persons on fixed incomes, for example, are more favorable toward controls than young family heads. The important point, though, is not these differences but the basic similarity of outlook shown by large numbers of Americans. It is as if they were saying, "Yes, we favor a free enterprise economy, but only when we can afford it." If current economic conditions suggest that industry can get along without governmental regulation, fine; otherwise it may be necessary from a pragmatic point of view to impose some controls on industry. This point of view, paradoxical though it may be, is not at all disturbing to most Americans. They still hold their principles, and they do not feel in any way compromised if "temporary" emergencies require action contrary to those principles.

THE PRIVATE POLITICS OF CONTROLS

It is easy enough to get the public aroused about some critical or emergency situation, and in this mood the public will generally be willing to support almost any action taken. The wage-price guidepost experience, as well as recent Gallup polls, suggests that this is true. It is easier, as any President would realize, to focus public attention on a few large, easily recognizable villains than it is to fragment public concern and squander Presidential prestige on a number of smaller, more diffuse targets.

The real test for wage and price regulation comes when there is no immediate crisis to justify actions taken to implement the controls. When guidelines become regulatory rules, the question of public support becomes much less critical for each individual application of the rules. In normal regulatory politics the voice of the regulated interest begins to sound clearly at this point, overshadowing the feeble voice of the general public. Most regulatory policies are, and must be, carried on largely in the absence of direct public attention, and their success from one case to the next presumably does not depend on public involvement.

Since there is nothing radically different in the idea of wage and price regulation that might require placing it in a special category, it is logical to assume that wage and price controls, after a brief period of operation, would be no more newsworthy than the decisions of, say, the SEC. Individual decisions would be of interest only to the individuals affected, even though the aggregate of decisions would certainly concern everyone.

For these reasons it is not sufficient to establish occasional public concern or occasional public acceptance of a policy measure such as wage and price control. To judge political feasibility accurately, it is necessary to see how special interests and the interests of the public at large agree with the general regulatory policy in question. This analysis has two parts. The first is a look at the actual effects of a wage and price control program: what kinds of economic costs and benefits does it impose and on what groups in the economy? Second is an examination of wage and price controls as a political issue involving both the general public and special interests. The purpose of this examination is to assess the lineup of political forces on the issue and to determine the likelihood that wage and price controls *could* be imposed and maintained in the American economy.

The guidepost experience offers some suggestions concerning the probable economic impact of wage and price controls. Guideposts were not applied universally. In fact, Presidents Kennedy and Johnson picked their targets with care, leaning heavily on price increases in large basic industries and allowing small business and service industries to set wages and prices at will, even though it was not true that the basic industries were the sole violators of the guideposts. In the short run, the price increases that hit consumers hardest were those in food items, personal services like haircuts, entertainment, and medical and dental bills.

Any actual program of wage and price regulation, like the guideposts, will probably begin with a recognition that across the board rules cannot and should not be applied. The history of federal minimum wage legislation illustrates the typical piecemeal development of economic regulation that would probably occur in the wage-price area. Initially minimum wage coverage was extended to only a few obviously interstate industries, and periodic expansions of coverage have taken very small steps into what might be considered intrastate business. The consistent aim of minimum wage exemptions has been to avoid harming small businesses and to avoid possibly unconstitutional encroachment on state regulatory prerogatives, and to this end the law establishes sales volume and employee size bounds below which minimum wage coverage does not apply.

In an emergency perhaps uniform wage and price ceilings could be imposed for the short run, but a continuing program

Table 7
The Economic Impact of Wage-Price Controls

Costs	*Who pays?*	*Benefits*	*Who gains?*
Loss of pricing freedom	Basic industries Labor unions	Lower prices	Consumers
		Slower inflation	Consumers
		Greater investment and general economic stability	Investors Banks

would, like minimum wage coverage, require more flexibility. A complete freeze on wage and price levels, with its temporary and emergency connotations, may succeed for a time, but it could hardly be a permanent solution.

In theory the Congress would set up universal rules and the burden of claiming special exceptions to them would be placed on the individual producer or labor union, but in practice the administering agency would almost immediately begin setting priorities and developing different standards. Further, with any luck at all, and with any degree of contact between industries and regulators, regulation should begin to assume the shape of the recommendations implicit in Table 6; that is, following an administrative policy similar to that for the guideposts. Finally, since inflation is being attacked at some of its major sources, it is probable that a large part of the wage and price increases forgone through regulation will be "made up" through greater stability in the purchasing power of wages and prices.

This analysis, which is only slightly optimistic, is summarized in Table 7. The table presents a perfect example of public interest regulation, where rather diffuse benefits are being provided for a large number of people through restriction of the activity of some smaller group of people. The regulated industries in Table 7 are not necessarily losing money, but simply giving up their power to make pricing and wage decisions in an irresponsible manner.

If all issues were simple enough to fit Table 7, the government certainly would be much more active than it is, and wage-price

Table 8
The Possible Political Impact of Wage-Price Controls

Costs	*Who pays?*	*Benefits*	*Who gains?*
Loss of pricing freedom	Basic industries Labor unions Small business Retailers Services	Lower prices	Consumers and their spokesmen
		Slower inflation	Consumers and their spokesmen
Lower profits	Basic industries Small business Retailers Services	Greater investment and general economic stability	Investors Banks and their spokesmen
Lower wages	Labor unions Other workers		
Socialistic	Conservatives Libertarians		

regulation would be part of that activity. The reasons for the repeated failure of wage-price regulation to pass Congress or to get approval from the executive branch can be expressed as political arguments added to the economic ones in Table 7. The speculative results of such an analysis are contained in Table 8. Note that all the differences between the two tables appear on the cost side, and that these added costs are diffuse in their impact. To put the argument very simply, any proposed extension of governmental regulation in the American economy will be perceived as threatening by large numbers of economic interests, and even some noneconomic ones, regardless of the probability or improbability of these threatened losses ever being incurred.

For wage and price controls the argument is even more pointed. Small business, professionals and some of the extractive industries in the United States are the strongest advocates of free enterprise ideology, as discussed in Chapter 3, and even though they would not be likely candidates for control they react ideologically against control in the abstract and against actual control applied to any sector at all. For them, the possibility of expanded governmental interference is alarming in itself, whatever the probability that they will actually suffer increased interference themselves.

Powerful wage maximizing unions and large profit maximizing corporations respond to the threat of controls in a more rational manner, being concerned about their own economic position as it may be worsened by regulation. Of course it would be possible to administer a wage-price regulating agency either to the advantage of unions or to the advantage of business, as critics have often alleged in the case of the National Labor Relations Board, but since either side may lose by the imposition of controls it is likely that they both will resist controls.

Finally, there almost certainly would be a number of individuals and groups opposing controls solely on ideological grounds. These groups, described as conservatives or libertarians in Table 8, often take stands on other political issues not related in any direct economic way to the question of wage and price policy. They would frequently be found defending state and local prerogatives against federal encroachment, for example, or taking patriotic stands in favor of American military strength and in opposition to foreign influence in the United States.

Many conservative political groups of course depend for their financial backing on individuals found elsewhere in Table 8—small business, for example, retailers and some professional services—but they should be considered separately because their ideological arguments go far beyond the economics of their members. Noted conservatives like William F. Buckley, Jr., for instance, are generally viewed as legitimate spokesmen for a political point of view and not as simply the mouthpiece of the American businessman.

THE PROGNOSIS FOR CONTROLS

The whole point behind the speculative analysis of Table 8 is that the policy process responds both to economics and to ideology and that all groups, whether directly economically affected or not, will have an impact on the actual course of wage and price policy. To draw any conclusions about the likelihood of wage and price controls being successfully imposed in the United States, one must estimate how each of the arguments in Table 8 is weighted into the policy process as a consequence of the political strength of its proponents. Such an analysis is risky at best, but since it lies at the heart of political-economic policy study some rough conclusions will be attempted here on the basis of the sparse evidence available.

Congress in general, and Republican congressmen in particular, are the primary political spokesmen for the interests of small businessmen and many professionals such as lawyers and doctors. The Republican party is also traditionally the home of big business interests while the Democratic party supposedly responds to the wishes of organized labor and, by extension, all workers. Regulatory agencies, to the extent that they will be involved in policy debates, generally speak for the interests of business, and more specifically small business. The Treasury Department and the Federal Reserve Board are important exceptions to the uniformity of the regulatory agencies, however, for they tend to speak for the interests of bankers and the federal government in economic stability.

With regard to consumers, representation is very fuzzy. No one speaks specifically for consumers, but anyone could do so. In recent years "consumerism" has become a political phenomenon, and major parties and many agencies have attempted to prove their superior credentials as consumer watchdogs. Precisely how consumer interests are to be weighted, therefore, depends on the current state of political payoff for doing battle in the name of the consumer.

One obvious peculiarity of the wage-price control issue is that labor and management find themselves on the same side of the argument. Much of the development of economic regulation in the past has depended on the possibility of playing these two against each other, and their alignment on this issue suggests a very strong coalition in opposition to any further imposition of controls. Galbraith's arguments have some relevance here, however. If his thesis concerning the decline of profit maximizing business and of labor unions is correct, then the "rational" resistance these two groups offer to wage and price controls should also decline in importance in the policy process.

Galbraith is unquestionably correct in arguing that the American economy is tending toward heavier concentrations of technological industry and service occupations, and these indisputable tendencies are certainly relevant for political prognosis. New technological industry stands on the sidelines when wage and price controls are mentioned because these controls, by and large, will not affect the economic situation of the technological industries or their employees.

The impact of the increase in service occupations is harder to estimate. If they become unionized, for instance, then they might continue to be a source of resistance to wage controls. If they do not become unionized, perhaps the safest prediction is that they will join Galbraith's technostructure on the sidelines.

The political future for wage-price controls, then, appears to be dominated by two major forces: the ideological opponents of controls and their Republican and congressional allies on the one side and the consumers and their sometime champions on the other. In the absence of economic crisis, voluntary and persuasive governmental supervision of wages and prices seems to be the most extreme policy feasible. In time of crisis, consumer sympathy may be strong enough to force temporary controls, but the long-run ideological resistance to such controls will probably continue undiminished for the foreseeable future. Any reformer bent on effective action against corporate and union "irresponsibility" may have to begin with reform of the dominant American free enterprise myth.

Notes

[1] For a brief summary see W. Carl Biven, *Economics and Public Policy* (Columbus: Merrill, 1966), pp. 148–77.

[2] *The New York Times,* December 1, 1969.

[3] Otto Eckstein and Gary Fromm, "Steel and the Postwar Inflation," Study paper No. 2, Joint Economic Committee Study of Employment, Growth and Price Levels, 1959.

[4] *Annual Report of the Council of Economic Advisers* (Washington, D.C.: U.S. Government Printing Office, 1962), pp. 185–90.

[5] Walter Heller, *New Dimensions of Political Economy* (Cambridge, Mass.: Harvard University Press, 1966), pp. 44–45.

[6] Arthur M. Okun, *The Political Economy of Prosperity* (Washington, D.C.: Brookings, 1970).

[7] *The New York Times,* May 25, 1969; November 12, 1969.

[8] John Kenneth Galbraith, *The New Industrial State* (Boston: Houghton Mifflin, 1967).

[9] Joint Economic Committee, Subcommittee on Economy in Government, hearings on The Acquisition of Weapons Systems, 1969, pp. 47, 58.

[10] *The New York Times,* March 6, 1971.

8

Distributing Rewards in the Affluent Society

Current American Rewards Policy

To most foreigners, the United States has always appeared immensely rich. It must also appear immensely wasteful to observers who come from societies forced to shepherd their financial resources. Even Americans, when they read the optimistic statistics provided eagerly by private and public agencies, get an impression of abundant wealth and expanding prosperity admitting of few exceptions and soft spots. Surely an economy with a gross national product of a trillion dollars, with employment levels running over 95 percent of the work force, with Social Security, unemployment compensation, extensive private pension and retirement plans, with free public education, with a graduated income tax, and with other marvels of modern political economy, should have no problem with the distribution of its rewards.

Foreign observers would also be surprised to discover that substantial poverty exists in the United States. "Why," they might say, "do you put up with poverty when you don't have to? In our countries we have always had to live with poverty—we just do not have the resources to eliminate it. But you have the resources and you don't use them. We don't understand it."

To these comments Americans are likely to reply that they have no conscious policy of poverty, but that they believe people should make their own way, and that personal wealth is the reward for hard work, skill, and inventiveness. No one has a right to live forever on the "public dole."

THE ROLE OF GOVERNMENT

These two views summarize much of the current debate on income distribution in the United States. The controversy has several parts: whether income distribution is an appropriate subject for direct governmental action; if there is a governmental role, what standards to use in allocating income; and finally whether the actual distribution of income is sufficiently out of step with some set of standards that positive governmental action is in fact required.

The first question is relatively simple to answer. There is unquestionably a governmental role in income distribution, if only because any governmental action or inaction in economic affairs has an effect on income distribution. Every economic system must distribute its products by some method or other, and every political system supports its accompanying economic system in the long run. Politics is at least an accomplice in the distribution of societal income, and it is really beside the point to argue that there is no political role in income distribution. That role, and therefore governmental responsibility, is inescapable.

Discussions of the proper distribution of goods and services in a society often resolve themselves into debates over income distribution alone. Of course, cash income in itself is only part of the larger question of the distribution of all goods and services. The actual pattern of income rewards may be an integral part of the purposes of a political-economic system or it may be merely a by-product of that system.

Income distribution is closely related to the distribution of the ultimate end products of the economy. Therefore, however cash income is treated in a particular system, it is an appropriate standard for judging the effects of systems. Very few modern economies provide substantial amounts of goods and services that are not valued in a common currency and exchanged in terms of that currency. Regardless of guiding philosophy, very few economies provide substantial portions of the needs and wants of citizens through some direct central allocation process. Even in socialist economies, where public revenues support a large variety of "free" health care and other forms of "in kind" assistance to citizens, these public programs are provided through income and sales taxation just as they are in predominantly free enterprise economies. Thus the forms of private income are retained, even if a large part of that income is in fact never available for spending by individuals.

At the other extreme, in free enterprise systems, cash income is the sole device for distributing production. Distribution of goods and services occurs through the choices made freely by individual consumers in markets. The United States, for example, is still close enough to a pure market economy (even if some of those markets are imperfectly competitive) that income distribution can be viewed as a sort of proxy for goods and services rewards. Food stamps, legal and counseling assistance, research and technical reports, and similar governmental programs; share cropping and other cooperative arrangements among individuals; free use of company automobiles and the like—these are all relatively unimportant in the overall pattern of rewards in the American economy, and will not be considered here.

With the pragmatic, skeptical attitude Americans take toward governmental intervention in the economy, they are not likely to rush to meddle with income distribution unless there is a persuasive reason to do so. If such reasons can be found, rhetoric and abstract argument probably will not prevail against them. Even the most persuasive calls to economic liberty will add little weight to the impact of observable poverty, for instance; nor will such arguments dramatize a poverty problem where poverty itself is nonexistent or isolated in a few small pockets. The questions to ask, then, are, "Can the average hard-working American earn enough to support his family?" "Are there substantial numbers who can not?" The right answer to either of these questions could be a persuasive reason for revamping present rewards policy.

THE NINETEENTH CENTURY'S WAR ON POVERTY

In the system of American economic beliefs, the emphasis on individualism and self-reliance produces some paradoxical conclusions. Speaking of the whole economy, Americans say "you can't get something for nothing." But focusing on the individual they say "you can get anything if you try hard enough." These seemingly contradictory beliefs are at the heart of the "war on poverty" as it was waged prior to the 1960s. This earlier war was the dominant social policy toward income distribution for all of the nineteenth century and, with few exceptions, for most of the twentieth century as well. As a policy, it required little positive governmental action, relying instead on individual initiative and generally benign neglect toward capitalist enterprise on the part of regulatory agencies.

The trillion dollar, full employment American economy provides obvious support for a casual assumption that the system has room for all. Historically the system *has* provided for nearly everyone. Even if self-made success was beyond the reach of many in the nineteenth century, the prosperity of the emerging captains of industry contributed to the average citizen's welfare through a kind of trickle-down process where wealth, and opportunities to achieve wealth, dispersed very widely from the successes of a few.

In the nineteenth century the war on poverty comprised skirmishes fought between each individual and circumstances. But the odds were not hopeless because circumstances were kind and individuals had a very good chance of gaining their share through the normal processes of economic expansion. Americans mistook the successful outcome of the majority of these skirmishes for a total victory—for many years we were blind to the income inadequacies of the few who could not make the American solution work. The inequities of the system opened it to criticism but for some time no one complained, and certainly few argued for a governmental responsibility in income maintenance.

Throughout the nineteenth century, and far into the twentieth, the welfare programs sponsored by local governments took their cue from the Elizabethan Poor Laws enacted in England nearly 300 years earlier. They aimed to help only the "deserving poor"—members of the work force temporarily out of work or persons not members of the work force by reason of permanent disability. Under this basic system the various categories of welfare assistance have developed, each one directed toward a specific group of persons judged deserving of a fixed level of income support.

General Assistance, provided by the states without federal aid, is the direct descendent of the Elizabethan system of local responsibility for the poor. Most of GA goes to recipients with permanent physical or mental disabilities who do not qualify for any of the federally supported categories.

The recipients of Old Age Assistance (OAA), Aid to the Blind (AB), Aid to the Permanently and Totally Disabled (APTD), and Aid to Families with Dependent Children (AFDC) are readily identified by the titles of the programs. The federal government pays part—50–83 percent—of the cost of these state programs through a matching formula based largely on per capita income in the state.

For the simple reason that they were intended to be only temporary relief or subsistence aid in extreme—and rare—cases, these five basic aid programs have never been noted for lavish benefit levels. In 1968, for example, only two states (New Jersey and Connecticut) provided income support for a family of four in AFDC greater than the poverty lines of $3,553 a year, while 26 states and the District of Columbia provided benefits less than two-thirds of this subsistence figure.

That New Jersey and Connecticut support AFDC recipients at levels higher than the national poverty line is largely a recognition of the higher-than-average living costs in those states: it is doubtful that even they fund AFDC at levels equal to the true subsistence costs for local recipients. At the opposite extreme benefits in 1968 ranged down to $660 per year, with thirteen states providing less than half of the national poverty line figure through AFDC.

Any tendency for the number of welfare recipients to increase has been met by economizing measures. This reaction, coupled with the understandable desires of welfare workers to help as many people as possible within the limited budgets of welfare departments, has led to restrictive and detailed administrative regulations in most states.

In principle, welfare recipients receive lump sum semimonthly aid checks to spend on their needs as they see fit; in practice the expenditure of aid money is often watched carefully by welfare department workers. In most county welfare agencies, for example, children's clothing allowances are doled out on a monthly basis by welfare caseworkers—$8 a month per child may be typical—and in extreme cases even such items as the number of new lipsticks a woman may buy each year are closely regulated. The furniture allowances in most instances are set so low that they will buy only used and rundown furniture, or very cheaply constructed new items.

Welfare recipients apparently must be reminded at every opportunity that they are subsisting on public beneficence, for most welfare systems—whether intentionally or not—force the recipient into the status of petitioner or supplicant. The paternalism of many caseworkers toward their clients is one indication of this attitude. Another is the abrogation of rights normally enjoyed by nonrecipients—until recently it was often the practice for welfare departments to stage midnight raids on the homes of some of their female recipients to see if a man who could be charged with part of the burden of child support might not secretly be present. Some 28 states and the District of Columbia still deny AFDC aid to male-headed families, regardless of income level, thus indirectly contributing to deception and family breakup.

The lion's share of the massive administrative expense of public assistance, over $250 million yearly for OAA, AB, and APTD alone, has been directed toward catching cheaters even though the percentage of fraudulent welfare cases has been small

—under 1 percent. The only ready explanation for this seemingly unproductive effort is the great symbolic importance attached to the concept of the "deserving poor" and the correspondingly great symbolic value in preventing escape of public funds into unworthy pockets. In fact, it was *federal* policy that until 1969 required verification of all welfare claims; to get federal matching funds states had to commit large portions of their welfare budgets to claims investigation.

In the twentieth century these old-style aid programs, even at low benefit levels, have not been miniscule in total dollar amounts, as Table 9 shows. Their expanding clientele points to the continuing fact of poverty even though eligible recipients number less than 40 percent of the poor. Actually, the number of people in poverty has been declining steadily while the proportion of the poverty population getting some kind of public assistance has increased, from about 18 percent in 1960 to over 38 percent in 1968. These figures might suggest that the basic aid programs are not really effective as antipoverty devices, and in fact that is the case. Table 10 shows the before and after pictures for public income transfers in 1965. The success rate, which is simply the ratio of those above the poverty line after payment to those below the line before payment, tells the story. For public assistance overall the success rate is 17 percent; for Social Security it is 46 percent. Neither group of

Table 9
Growth of Public Assistance, 1950–69

	Number of recipients (millions)	*Amount of payments (billions)*	*Percent of total payments*		
			OAA	*AFDC*	*APTD, AB, GA*
1950	6.1	$2.4	62%	23%	15%
1955	5.8	2.5	59	24	17
1960	7.1	3.3	50	30	20
1965	7.8	4.0	40	41	19
1969	10.4	6.5	27	53	20

Source: U.S. Department of Health, Education, and Welfare figures, cited in *Improving the Public Welfare System* (New York: Committee for Economic Development, 1970).

Table 10
The Impact of Public Transfers, 1965

Recipient category	*Any program*[a] percent before	*Any program*[a] poor[b] after	*Social Security* percent before	*Social Security* poor after	*Public Assistance* percent before	*Public Assistance* poor after
Unrelated individuals under 65	68%	47%	82%	58%	95%	79%
Unrelated individuals 65 and over	87	58	84	56	99	86
Families						
Male head						
Under 65	24	14	26	15	58	47
65 and over	63	21	59	20	81	56
Female head						
Under 65	66	48	52	28	89	78
65 and over	51	30	46	26	66	45
All households	55	31	59	32	81	67

Source: Mollie Orshansky, "The Shape of Poverty in 1966," *Social Security Bulletin*, March 1968.

[a] Includes programs in addition to Social Security and Public Assistance.
[b] "Poor" is defined as below the poverty line.

programs succeeds as often as half the time, with the sole exception of Social Security for families headed by a male over 65. For all other groups the public income transfer system, including public assistance, is obviously inadequate.

POVERTY AND POVERTY LINES

The remarkable thing about poverty in the United States is that it has been declining steadily despite the inadequacy of basic aid. A quick glance at the poverty percentages, shown in Table 11, would encourage even the most hard-pressed taxpayer. Obviously, great progress has been made in the past decade in eliminating poverty, and that largely without direct governmental assistance. Many Americans are leaving poverty because of individual hard work and aggregate economic prosperity; about fourteen million of them did so between 1959 and 1968.

Table 11
The Poverty Population, 1959–68

	Number below poverty line (millions)	*Percent of population below poverty line*
1959	39.5	22%
1960	39.9	22
1961	39.6	22
1962	38.6	21
1963	36.4	19
1964	36.1	19
1965	33.2	17
1966	30.4	16
1967	27.8	14
1968	25.4	13

Source: U.S. Bureau of the Census, *Current Population Reports*, Series P-20, No. 189 (August 18, 1969).

The easy conclusion that Table 11 suggests is that the old-style poverty war is working, and its apparently remarkable success places recent concern about poverty in a strange light. It seems that the American public's discovery of poverty has come about not because of the number of poor people, but because of the tax burden of supporting them. Americans are beginning to realize the full cost of poverty, and they do not like it.

Unfortunately these optimistic figures for poverty decline are misleading in several respects. Twenty-five million poor people (in 1968; see Table 11) is not in itself a small number, but the current poverty line definition tends to underestimate greatly the extent of the poverty problem. As calculated by the Social Security Administration, an urban family is poor if it has less than the annual income necessary to buy food (about 75¢ a day per person in 1966) on the assumption that food expenses should be no more than one-third of the total family budget. Thus the poverty line for an urban family of four is $\$0.75 \times 4 \times 3 \times 365 =$ roughly \$3,300.

Based on family size, place of residence, and food costs, the poverty line represents a basic subsistence level rather than even a modest version of the consumer's "American dream." As a result it does not keep pace with the rise of general living standards. Between 1959 and 1966, a highly prosperous period when unemployment fell markedly and production rose to new record levels, the poverty line rose only from $3,100 to $3,335 for an urban family of four, or an increase of 9 percent. During the same seven years the median family income in the United States rose 37 percent, from $6,070 to $8,340.[1]

Thus the family that manages to stay just above the poverty line will find itself officially nonpoor while in fact it slips farther and farther below the average standard of living in the United States. On their television sets they will see daily glimpses of a lifestyle that increasingly diverges from the reality of their lives, and they will suffer a form of "relative poverty" or "psychological poverty" as a result. This kind of poverty is not often recognized because the affluent majority in America sets up a double standard, viewing subsistence as an adequate level for the poor while itself looking to a standard far beyond this basic minimum.

A more realistic estimate of the number of people who are "relatively poor" would be the Social Security Administration's concept of "near poverty" which was $4,700 for an urban family of four in 1969, or the "lower living standard" of the Bureau of Labor Statistics, which was about $6,400 for the same family in 1969. The figures here would begin to be embarrassingly large—44.8 million or 23.1 percent poor and near poor in 1966, for example. These figures all emphasize one point very clearly—the idea of an income floor near the poverty line is not at all a radical proposal for the United States. Such a floor would represent a very minor modification in the overall distribution of income, only somewhat greater in redistributive impact than some of the recent tax reform legislation, and obviously very far indeed from income equality.

The poverty figures also imply that overall economic prosperity can go on lifting people out of poverty indefinitely. If the poverty trends in Table 11 are blithely projected into the future it would seem that poverty (by the minimal subsistence income definition) could be eliminated almost entirely by the late 1970s. But such a conclusion ignores the marked changes in the composition of the poor over the past decade. In fact, the expanding economy of the 1960s took most of the easy cases out of poverty through the "trickle-down" mechanism, leaving behind the real hard core of poverty. Table 12 shows this composition change graphically for selected groups of the population. While the total number of people under the poverty line fell by almost 36 percent between 1959 and 1968, this decrease was concentrated in a few categories of the population, most notably in male-headed families, where the number in poverty was roughly halved. In nearly every other category—persons over 65, nonwhite persons, female headed households—the poverty decline was substantially less. The most dramatic changes took place in nonwhite female headed families, where the number of poor people *increased* by nearly as great a percentage as the percentage of overall decrease.

It is particularly interesting to note that the categories of increasing poverty are precisely those (OAA and AFDC) accounting for most of the public assistance spending inceases over the past decade. If more evidence is needed that the old-style war on poverty is not working, these figures certainly provide it. Preliminary 1970 poverty figures confirm this picture: in that year 13 percent of all Americans, 25.5 million people, were still in poverty.[2]

Table 12
Changes in the Composition of Poverty, 1959–68

	Change in millions of persons	*Change in percent*
All persons	−14.1	−36
Nonwhite persons	−3.0	−27
Persons 65 and over	−1.1	−19
Unrelated individuals	−0.2	−5
Persons in female-headed households		
Total	0.0	0
Children	+0.3	+6
Nonwhites	+0.7	+21
Nonwhite children	+0.6	+35

Source: Figures cited in Committee for Economic Development, "Improving the Public Welfare System," April 1970, p. 27.

WHO ARE THE POOR?

If the current poverty programs are not working, even with categoric aid, full employment, job training, Social Security, and a host of other public and private income maintenance devices, something more must be done. But exactly what is to be done is not an abstract question. It is rooted in the precise character of those Americans who are in poverty and, equally important, the political acceptability of the various proposals for income maintenance made since the emergence of poverty as a public issue in the mid 1960s. The characteristics of the poor are important in that they reveal a lot about the effectiveness of various poverty solutions in relation to the apparent causes of poverty. At the same time, public acceptability is important because public preferences and prejudices will generally shape the political response to an issue of general concern like poverty.

The first thing we know about the poor, even before consulting statistical evidence, is that they are a mixed lot, being poor to differing degrees and for different reasons. The public image of the poor encompasses primarily people "on welfare" and, within that group, primarily nonwhite mothers receiving AFDC benefits. But as shown before, this image springs mainly from the rapid increase in this particular program in the past decade (see Table 9) and does not reflect an accurate picture of the poor in America.

Table 13 presents one profile of the poor, showing a number of ways of dividing the total group. It is immediately apparent from this table that there are several distinguishable categories of poverty rather than one uniform group. The table also explodes some popular stereotypes about poverty: the typical poor person is a white child in a large family, living in an urban area, with a male family head who works at least part time. But even this picture, although it is more accurate than popular images of poverty, still obscures the varieties of poverty and clouds an issue which is already in great need of clarification.

Table 13
A Profile of the Poor, 1966

	Number in millions
Total poor persons	29.6
In families	24.8
Family heads	6.1
Children	12.5
Other family members	6.2
With male heads	17.7
With female heads	7.1
White families	16.3
Nonwhite families	8.5
Unrelated individuals	4.8
Under 65	2.1
65 and over	2.7

Source: Mollie Orshansky, "The Shape of Poverty in 1966," *Social Security Bulletin*, March 1968.

Some clarity can be brought to the poverty picture by distinguishing four classes of the poor:

Aged poor. Poor because of inadequate private retirement benefits, inadequate Social Security benefits, high medical expenses, and so forth.

Disabled poor. Poor because of inability to work (permanent physical or mental handicaps and the like) or because work is considered unsuitable (mothers of preschool children, for example).

Working poor. Poor because of low skill levels, sporadic job availability, low wages, or large families.

Nonworking poor. Poor because of low skill levels, shortage of jobs, because they are undependable, labor force dropouts, etc.

Because the income status of Americans is so closely related to directly earned income, and most of that from direct employment, it does not distort the poverty picture very much to focus on families and on the one or two wage earners in each family. As Table 13 shows, about 84 percent of all poor people live in families. The important point, then, is that an average of three additional people are poor for each earner of inadequate income. They have no choice but to be poor, unless they join the labor force themselves.

So if families are characterized according to family heads, the total of approximately 6.1 million poor families in 1966 divides as follows (see Table 14):

Aged heads: 1.5 million poor families
Disabled heads (ill): 0.4 million poor families
Disabled heads (other reasons): 0.7 million poor families
Working heads: 3.3 million poor families
Nonworking heads: 0.2 million families

In short, more than half of the poor families in the United States in 1966 were poor even though family heads (and possibly other family members) were in the work force. The American dream has some gaping holes, for here are willing workers unable to earn enough to support their families even at the poverty line, much less at an adequate standard of living.

Any number of reasons can be advanced for this startling statistic. About 1.5 million of these poor families had family heads who worked only part time during 1966, and if no other income came into the family such part-time unemployment could drop a family into poverty. Perhaps the most obvious reason, however, is large family size. An income that would be adequate for a family of four may plunge a family of six or seven into poverty. The statutory minimum wage of $1.60 an hour, for example, if earned forty hours a week for fifty weeks a year, or a total of 2,000 hours a year, will support a family of four near the poverty line but it would obviously be inadequate for any larger family. The 2.2 million poor families with three or more children, and especially the 900,000 poor families with five or more children, bulk large in the poverty population.

Table 14
Poor Families, 1966

	Number in millions
Total families	6.1
No children	2.2
1 or 2 children	1.7
3 or 4 children	1.2
5 or more children	0.9
Farm families	0.5
Nonfarm families	5.6
Income level	
Under $1,000	1.2
$1,000–1,999	2.5
$2,000–2,999	1.2
$3,000–4,999	1.1
Over $5,000	0.1
Male head under 65	
Not working; illness	0.3
Not working; other reasons	0.2
Working at least part time	2.5
In military service	0.1
Female head under 65	
Not working; illness	0.1
Not working; other reasons	0.7
Working at least part time	0.8

Source: Mollie Orshansky, "The Shape of Poverty in 1966," *Social Security Bulletin*, March 1968.

Since wage rates in the United States are not set in relation to the family size of a wage earner, but in relation to his productive usefulness, the father of five children will receive no more than the father of two children for his labor unless he is also a more productive worker. The typical survival strategy for the poor or near-poor family with five children is for the head to hold two jobs or for other members of the family to work, so that the family has two incomes rather than one. The impact of this desperate measure on family life can be easily imagined.

Another startling fact about poverty, and a fact that contradicts some popular notions, is that only a very small proportion of the poor are in poverty because they are lazy. In 1966 less than 200,000 poor families had a male head who was not working and had no plausible excuse for his idleness. Adding unrelated individuals under age 65 who were not in the labor force in 1966 (about 800,000) gives a maximum of about 1.5 million people poor because of unspecified reasons. For some of these people, permanent disability may explain their absence from the labor force; thus this estimate of the loafing poor probably overstates their numbers. But even 1.5 million out of a total of almost thirty million poor in 1966, or just 5 percent, does not make the case that there is a vast army of the poor eager to live off the public dole. Poverty, and the status of public debtor, is simply not that desirable to the average American, rich or poor.

How Income Is Distributed

THE REDISTRIBUTION ISSUE

Income distribution, at first glance, is a strange area for governmental involvement in a predominantly capitalist economy. Under capitalist assumptions, no greater or lesser public benefit derives from one pattern of income distribution or another, and the abstract benefits of maximum production and productive capacity occur naturally without governmental interference. In a capitalist economy, also, there are no "villains" whose villainous activity must be regulated, for individual self-seeking is encouraged as the only sure route to overall social benefit.

But if the United States has a capitalist economy, it must be possible to find some justifications for intervention because a variety of governmental programs in the United States do in fact redistribute income as a conscious aim of policy. Apparently income redistribution in the "welfare" sense is largely a symbolic issue, because redistribution itself has been practiced for many years while at the same time being vehemently rejected as a general policy in the United States. Perhaps a look at some of the existing programs will suggest practical justifications for "welfare" oriented redistribution.

Minimum wage legislation is one case of income policy in the United States. Since 1938, when the program began, it has been defended on a variety of grounds. The periodic congressional hearings investigating the wisdom of rate increases or coverage extensions always produce a catalogue of arguments pro and con, and often a single witness will invoke several of these standard arguments in support of his position:

1. As a simple welfare measure—they supposedly express society's concern that all full time working men be paid enough to meet the basic subsistence needs of their families;

2. As an equity measure, they help to prevent wage cutting and wage differentials that are not related to differences in skill and performance;

3. As a positive measure of economic policy: wage increases at the bottom levels, it is alleged, increase total purchasing power in the economy and thus eventually contribute to greater prosperity for all Americans.

Veterans' benefits are another sizable part of the income redistribution picture. Originally a relatively modest program of disability compensation, benefits have expanded at the urging of veterans' organizations and their powerful lobby to include the GI Bill for World War II and Korean war veterans and the Cold War GI Bill, which extended similar educational aid, job training, and job placement benefits to veterans of our peacetime armed forces.

"Nothing is too good for our boys," America says, and certainly veterans' benefits will continue to claim a high place in national priorities for a long time. The reason is simply equity, for the most part. Veterans are "deserving." They have served their country, and now their country owes them compensation. More important, the burden of providing national defense for all, and the associated risks of injury and death, falls on only a few, even under a full wartime mobilization like that of World War II. Thus the equity argument for veterans' benefits rests at bottom on the nature of national defense as a public good.

A third example of governmental income redistribution is agricultural price supports. Actually they are just one representative of a large class of subsidy programs, many of which were discussed in Chapter 4, but price supports also have a number of possible justifications. Similar to the minimum wage argument, the rationale for price support refers to farmers both as a deserving group in themselves and as an important link in overall national prosperity.

It should not be surprising that income redistribution has a variety of justifications, since there is no overall rewards policy unifying the various programs which redistribute income and since each individual program has its own pragmatic ad hoc origin and its own political supporters and detractors. The appeals to principle and the attempts at justification are largely that—appeals and justifications—but they are crucial for analysis because they reveal some central notions in American thinking about income and its proper distribution.

ARGUMENTS FOR REDISTRIBUTION

Two common themes run through the three areas of income policy above, the themes of "public benefit" and the "deserving beneficiary." Using the terms developed in chapter 6, these themes correspond to the subsidy situation and the public good situation, and they may serve as a basis for more general and acknowledged income policies.

But there is one serious problem that arises immediately: most of the proposed recipients of any welfare program are not performing indispensable economic activities, and many are not performing any economic activity at all (except consuming). The justifications here, it would seem, must be either feeble or quite indirect.

Several arguments have been advanced with regard to welfare recipients. One is a negative argument that says simply that the poor are no less deserving than anyone else. Another argument is that of the foreign observer: you can afford it, so why not? A third approach refers to the hidden costs involved in allowing any substantial group in society to remain poor, and a related point of view stresses the positive benefits for the entire economy of bringing up the economic level of its bottom fraction. Whether or not any of these arguments is completely persuasive is not important; the purpose of presenting them here is simply to show that income redistribution can be intellectually respectable.

The first argument in support of positive governmental action to redistribute income grows out of assumptions about the real sources of most private wealth today. The American myth of individual advancement through the exercise of frontier virtues like hard work, perseverance, thrift, inventiveness, and perhaps luck has nearly outlived its usefulness as a description of American realities. But for many years this frontier myth was literally true for the large majority of Americans. Not all of them followed that route, nor were they all ultimately successful in converting its strictures into money, but enough were successful to maintain nearly universal adherence to the myth.

Today there are many fewer of these elemental paths to personal success, but there are a number of quicker ways to make a million that usually seduce the would-be economic frontiersman. Most of the appealing opportunities for making money these days depend on the existence of an elaborate framework of social and economic institutions largely preserved and supervised through continuous governmental action. Governments have always defined and protected private property, of course, and certainly without property rights the accumulation of economic wealth would be much more risky and uncertain than it now is. But even beyond this minimal kind of encouragement of private enterprise most governments—including the American—regulate, stabilize, subsidize, and otherwise protect a number of opportunities for profit making, and in each of these areas governmental aid is often indispensable.

For instance, the inventor who creates a new manufacturing process, patents it, borrows funds to set up a small business, begins to export his product, and eventually "goes public" by offering the public shares of stock in his company is obviously relying on the government either directly or indirectly all along the line. His federal patent is designed to encourage him to invent, and it protects his right to exploit his inventions for a certain period of time unhampered by imitators. His bank loan for initial working capital may come through the Small Business Administration or it may come through regular banking channels, but banking channels would not be nearly so regular and credit probably would not be so readily available if governmental banking regulation and governmental credit policy were not in effect.

Exports would also be more difficult if the federal government did not encourage them and if federal negotiation had not regularized foreign trade business and (in some cases) lowered the tariff barrier facing American goods in foreign ports. Finally, the businessman can expect a ready market for his stock in part because SEC regulation of securities issues and trading has created a stock market which enjoys broad public confidence.

This involvement, as extensive as it is, does not even begin to mention the immense governmental impact of procurement programs at the federal, state, and local levels and their direct and indirect stimulative effects on private business. The point could be labored at great length, but it should be obvious enough from this simple example that the economic links between business and government are extensive and various. Governmental economic intervention is not intentionally punitive or restrictive to the legitimate profit-oriented businessman. Much of the time governmental regulation aims to make his economic ventures simpler, less risky, and more profitable. This simple fact often gets overlooked in the rhetoric surrounding governmental "meddling" and it is worth noting again.

Further, the SEC, the Small Business Administration, and all other governmental agencies directly or indirectly aiding business do not act exclusively to benefit the businessman. Every one of these agencies has a clearly formulated and at least partly valid public interest justification for its existence, and its promotional activity or its benevolent regulation is taken in the name of the general public. A logical conclusion to this line of reasoning, but an understandably controversial one, is that very few individuals today can lay exclusive claim to the use and disposal of the income they receive.

Carrying the argument one step farther, it can also be said that some of the income inequalities in any system where governments are active must be the result of government policy rather than of differences of individual merit or work effort. Thus, if the extent of income inequality is sufficiently great there may be a logical argument for corrective income redistribution. Specifically, those individuals who benefit disproportionately from existing governmental rewards policy have a duty to provide for their own present and retirement needs, while individuals who are hurt by present policy to the point of inability to meet their income requirements have a valid claim against the general public for assistance.

Most people have some form of this argument in mind when they say, "Society has a responsibility to help those less fortunate," but their expressions are only rhetorical unless they really believe that "society" has some important effect on who is fortunate and who is not. Most people find it hard to believe that they are beneficiaries of government policy, and the ad hoc development of the American welfare state has substantially obscured the extent of individual dependence on social and governmental institutions.

The second argument ("we can afford it") is simply expressed. The American economy has reached the point where there is in fact enough to go around. Disregarding the claims of public needs, there is enough personal income in the United States that minimum adequate living standards could be guaranteed to every citizen if some amount of income redistribution took place. Few Americans realize how rapidly and dramatically American prosperity has increased since the 1930s. In 1969 disposable personal income was $630 billion, or $3,098 per person. Even after allowances are made for changes in the purchasing power of the dollar, this figure is twice that of 1941 or any previous year. Somewhere between these two dates it became theoretically possible to achieve adequate income levels for everyone in the United States, a situation never before known in this country and probably unknown in any other industrialized country in the world before that time. Abundance argues for the substitution of an assumption of plenty for the often-voiced assumption of scarcity, but in reality so sweeping a change of assumptions would require a long period of time because it challenges the fundamental beliefs of many Americans.

Finally, a pair of related arguments refer to the costs of poverty for society at large. Michael Harrington, in his book *The Other America,* documented for many Americans the fate of a portion of society they did not know about and sometimes preferred not to know about.[3] Their ignorance, whether calculated or accidental, was also ignorance of the costs of poverty, for certainly these costs would have aroused widespread concern faster than humanitarian feelings could. (But to be completely fair, the costs of poverty are diverse, usually hidden in their impact, and relatively minor when considered separately. Only when they are discovered and added up is their full significance apparent.)

Any concrete estimate of the social cost of poverty must be speculative in large part, but most estimates have been close to the cost of expensive antipoverty proposals—about $20 to $25 billion a year. More important than the dollar amount, however, is the range of expenses encompassed by the total figure. First is the productivity lost through the unemployment and underemployment of human resources that accounts for much of poverty. Government statistics are outrageously optimistic in their picture of slum labor conditions because they do not take account of labor force dropouts. The Bureau of Labor Statistics calculates the unemployment rate by counting the number of people actively seeking work and dividing by the number in the labor force (those working plus those seeking work). But in slum areas especially, there are large numbers of men of working age who are not seeking work because they feel the labor market offers them no opportunities.

Not until 1969 did the Bureau begin to gather data on this phenomenon; in one spot survey in New York City a total labor force of 111,000 included 5,600 unemployed while another 7,000, not in the labor force, had "labor market adjustment problems" of temporary or permanent character and were not currently working.[4]

Underemployment of resources is also a serious problem even for members of the work force. Failures in the educational system become failures in the work force, even if they work full time, because their potential abilities are never developed and exploited. The extent of these failures cannot easily be measured; any calculation must include both the loss to society and the loss to the individual himself.

Also to be reckoned in the social cost of poverty is the loss of property and life resulting from illegal activities of the poor. Lack of legitimate opportunities for advancement in the labor market leads many of the poor into crime, and the burden of actual crime victimization is shared widely through higher insurance rates, installation costs of alarm and home protection devices, even karate instruction which might not otherwise be needed. If poverty were eliminated tomorrow crime would not disappear, of course, and insurance rates would not fall to zero, but in the long run substantial and widespread benefits in these areas would be felt.

The poor also fall victim to businesses that promise large immediate returns for little cost, whether legal—high interest consumer credit on poor quality merchandise, for example—or illegal—the numbers game. Because these are socially wasteful expenses arising out of the despair of the poor rather than from their real desires, they should be viewed as social liabilities rather than social benefits. Again, to eliminate poverty would not immediately put out of business those who prey upon the poor, but it would ultimately rechannel some of their energies into more socially valued enterprise.

WORK INCENTIVES AND THE VALUE OF WORK

Another philosophical issue that always comes to the fore in discussions of welfare reform is the concept of the value of work. If it is assumed that work will continue to be necessary for the large majority of Americans in the near future, then any poverty solution must take the work ethic and work incentives into account. But simply saying "the work ethic must be applied" is not the end of the story.

To understand the nineteenth century ethic of hard work and individual success it is necessary to appreciate its major unstated assumption that the work is worth doing. Labor that contributes directly and immediately to personal subsistence or to personal wealth certainly is worth doing, but it should not be so easily assumed that every kind of labor today meets this criterion. It can be argued that the only justification for elevating self-reliance and hard work to a social policy solution for individual welfare is the assumption that everyone can find, not just a job, but a job that offers adequate pay, personal rewards, and advancement opportunities. Dishwashing jobs, street construction jobs, and the like, even if they did pay a living wage (which often they do not) can hardly be said to afford advancement opportunities or great personal satisfactions. And yet these jobs are socially useful.

Here is the dilemma: there are socially useful jobs to be done but which nevertheless require such low skill levels that their wages will not support even subsistence, much less allow the worker to be a full participating member in society. By and large it was social policy up to the 1960s to raise the wage levels of some of these jobs by statute and to hope that they would be filled by the generally large supply of laborers whose skill level did not allow them to compete for better jobs. Those who did have a job, regardless of its wage rate, were presumed to be self-sufficient, while those who could not find work of any kind were aided by the stopgap measures discussed earlier in this chapter.

This approach might be amended to say that if truly rewarding jobs are not available there is no honor and no justice in requiring individuals to fend for themselves on jobs that are demeaning and do not pay adequate wages. To insist that the individual forced to take such a job should be content is to make a mockery of the notion of the value of work. It is nonsensical to insist that an individual value a job just because it is socially necessary.

Governmental policy based on this assumption can also be faulted for attempting to enforce virtue. For if the virtues of work are really that basic and formative in the American culture, they must be inbred and subconscious, and not in need of enforcement by law. Conversely, a person reaching maturity who would rather loaf than work for a living must be counted a failure of the educational system. He can be made to work if he has no available means of free support, but rarely can he be coerced into assuming the dominant values of society. Furthermore, the apparent virtue or lack of virtue in any individual does not affect his income needs and presumably should not affect his treatment by a welfare system.

The argument here is not that people do not have to work. In this view a welfare system can be based on the desirability of work, but at the same time it should recognize that there may be a shortage of adequately paying jobs and that the private job market is not the whole solution even for the welfare of those who are able bodied and willing to work. In addition the presumption in such a welfare system should be against attaching any stigma to the status of welfare recipient. Because of the "undeserved" character of much of the income earned in the modern economy, the individual should not be held culpable for failure to provide for his own needs (assuming he is willing to work) any more than the self-provident individual should be allowed to claim superior virtue. For those who have exhausted the means of the economic market and are still in need, welfare assistance should be a matter of simple right.

Most arguments for redistribution and welfare reform in the United States have become partly irrelevant since, for whatever reasons, a consensus has emerged that existing welfare aid programs are insufficient and in need of major overhaul or outright replacement. But this consensus does not imply general agreement on any fixed set of principles, and conflicts in the areas just explored will still shape the development of welfare programs or their replacements. If it is recognized, for example, that there is some element of public benefit or public good involved in a solution to income poverty then there will probably be agreement on some kind of governmental responsibility for income maintenance. But this agreement need not include the notion of income security as an individual right, and real political conflict is certain to begin when these technical questions of detail come up for a definite decision.

Toward a Poverty Solution

Even in the face of welfare controversy, the failure of system-level solutions (full employment and trickle down) and the inadequacies of stopgap measures (categoric aid) have certainly opened the way in public acceptance for some kind of effective attack on continuing income inadequacy. Of necessity a variety of approaches will be used such as job training, minimum wage increases, and the like, as well as system-level policies, but each of these has its own limits. Job-finding approaches, for instance, do not deal with all kinds of poverty, and they have inherent limits determined by the needs of society for various kinds of labor. A policy solution, then, requires finding the additional measures necessary to fill the large gaps in existing income policy.

A VARIETY OF STRATEGIES

The fact of diversity among the poor strongly suggests a diversity of approaches for dealing with poverty. The point of examining different poverty groups earlier in this chapter was to suggest solutions tailored to the specific causes of poverty for each group. Across-the-board solutions, while they may work to eliminate poverty, may not be most efficient for certain types of poverty problems. For most existing poverty programs there is also a sizable entrenched bureaucracy that would unquestionably resist the imposition of new rules on its programs, much less accept the replacement of those cherished programs with wholly new ones. The pragmatic bias in American policy making thus calls for an incremental strategy, paring the problem down as far as possible and then attempting to make minimum changes in existing policy to solve the problem that remains.

In the first place, then, the over-65 group can be removed since they are already covered by Social Security and by OAA. The problem here, to the extent that OASDHI recipients are still poor, is one of closing the few remaining gaps of coverage and of keeping the benefit levels high enough. To summarize data in Table 10, OASDHI does well in eliminating poverty for families where the head is over 65: 67 percent of the 9.1 million households headed by a person over 65 would have been poor without Social Security while only 35 percent of those households were still poor after receiving Social Security benefits due the household head. The income problems of the aged are neither terribly large nor terribly far from solution, nor are these problems at the focus of public concern. That focus is on other poverty classes.

From an economic standpoint the poverty of the "disabled" group is also readily amenable to solution. For the family whose head is temporarily out of work because of illness, the obvious solution is better and more complete sick pay and workmen's compensation coverage. At present these programs are largely private, financed out of the general revenues of employers and subject to variation from employer to employer. Except for federal government employees and longshoremen and harbor workers, workmen's compensation is regulated under state laws and is therefore subject to state-to-state variations. Again the problem is one of adequacy of level and completeness of coverage. Gaps in state coverage could perhaps be closed by a fall-back federal program or by establishment of federal minimum standards. If these changes were made, the welfare of the family whose head was temporarily ill would then be determined simply by the income the family head would normally expect to earn, supplemented by the earnings of any other members of the household. Similar gaps and similar correctives can be proposed for the permanently disabled since they are, in theory, already covered by state programs.

Female-headed families with small children pose a less clearcut policy problem although they also are treated under existing policy. A question not entirely resolved under AFDC is whether the heads of these families should work or not. It is generally accepted that mothers of preschool children need not work, but when their children go to school the mothers could go back to work. Even mothers of preschool children can work if they take advantage of a day care center, but this program has always been voluntary because not enough day care facilities have been available to meet even the voluntary demand.

Whether mothers of preschool children, or of children of any age, must work is not directly a question for a poverty policy to answer. The broader point at issue here is one of society's investment in its children and the expected role of women in child rearing and training. Poverty policy must respond to the income needs of nonworking female family heads only when they are considered deserving aid recipients. This principle would mean that AFDC should be funded at a level at least equal to subsistence needs and that day care should be provided to the extent that it allows women to work and earn part of their income needs. Day care facilities may additionally be made available to other women if general social policy declares that women should be free to choose careers outside the home if they wish.

THE WORKING POOR

The working poor remain the primary focus of new antipoverty effort. For this group the existing categoric welfare programs have little to offer since they are geared to recipients not in the labor force. Most of the recommendations for aiding the working poor fall back on job training, job placement, education, and similar solutions. The available evidence seems to indicate that the working poor do not lack the desire to work, but that their objective chances are often discouraging enough to lead them into high rates of absenteeism and tardiness. In brief, it appears that the poverty problem of the working poor will respond only to long-range and basic solutions.

The job of analysis can be simplified, then, by limiting the discussion to some kind of income strategy. Such a strategy will certainly be needed in the short run until education, training, and other approaches take hold, and probably some basic income supplement program will be needed indefinitely. But what kind of an income program is needed?

Table 15 presents some characteristics of three income maintenance plans that figure prominently in current discussions. On each characteristic the three plans offer a range of alternatives, but no plan is obviously superior. Advocates of a children's allowance must admit that their proposal is inefficient as an antipoverty de-

Table 15
Three Income Maintenance Plans

	Orshansky's $25 children's allowance	*Lampman's flat income guarantee*	*Tobin's "L 33" negative rates plan*
Target group	Families with children	Low income households	Low income households
Categories of the poor helped	All in families with children	All	All
Fraction of the poor lifted out of poverty	Approximately 36%	100%	All with incomes greater than half of the poverty line
Total cost	$11 billion	$25 billion	$12–15 billion
Fraction of the cost going to the poor	37%	100%	70%
Incentives	Same as under present tax structure	Marginal tax rate of 100%	Marginal tax rate of $33\frac{1}{3}$%

Sources: Mollie Orshansky, "The Shape of Poverty in 1966," *Social Security Bulletin* 31 (March 1968): 3–32; Robert J. Lampman, statement in hearings before the Joint Economic Committee, U.S. Congress, June 1968; James Tobin, Joseph A. Pechman, and Peter M. Mieszkowski, "Is a Negative Income Tax Practical?" *Yale Law Journal* 77 (November 1967): 1–27.

vice—less than half of the payments go to poor families and for many recipients benefit levels would not be adequate.

Critics of an income guarantee that just fills each family's poverty gap would concede its efficiency, but they would claim that a 100 percent marginal tax rate on earned income is pretty steep. Why should any guarantee recipient work to supplement his income—or to get out of poverty—if in fact he cannot keep any of his earnings? What about wage earners currently making $3,700 a year? Will they quit work and take the guarantee instead? Isn't $25 billion a large price tag for aiding the poor, and then only by bringing them just up to the poverty line? Further, this cost estimate is about double the total poverty gap—it explicitly assumes many of the poor will stop working entirely to take the guarantee.

Negative income tax advocates view it as the best compromise plan, but they must admit that an adequate minimum guarantee level will be inefficient: it will result in substantial benefits for people who are not poor. (Currently, AFDC operates as a kind of negative income tax, with a disregard of the first $30 of earned income monthly and a benefit reduction of 67 cents for each earned dollar over that—in effect, a 67 percent marginal tax rate. But AFDC benefits are cut off when a family reaches an income level near subsistence, so that few officially nonpoor benefit from this program.)

These four design criteria for a welfare system emerge from these criticisms:

1. Adequacy. The plan should guarantee at least a subsistence income.
2. Incentive. It should encourage work to supplement or supplant aid payments.
3. Economy. Total cost should be as low as possible.
4. Efficiency. It should aid only the poor, and should pay them only as much as necessary.

Some tradeoffs among these criteria are possible, but no scheme can be devised to satisfy all four criteria at once. A $50 monthly children's allowance would raise 64 percent of the poor out of poverty, for example, but only 29 percent of its $28 billion cost would go to poor families. The amount of benefit going to the nonpoor can be decreased in a negative income tax scheme, but only by lowering the guarantee level or raising the marginal tax rate. (At the extreme of a 100 percent marginal rate a negative rates plan becomes simply a flat income guarantee, so these schemes are not fundamentally different from each other.)

For political reasons, family allowance advocates often play up the supposed defect of dispersed aid distribution by arguing that aid based not on poverty status but on family size alone will unite society rather than dividing it and will blur the stigma of aid receipt. But people without children may not readily accept this argument because they will not be recipients. Parents of small families may resent the aid received by large families, and nearly everyone, including recipients, will resent the total cost of any very large family allowance program.

The issue of tax equity further complicates matters. A negative income tax plan imposes marginal tax rates higher than any except those applied to the very highest income levels. Is it equitable to tax earned income for the aid recipient at a marginal rate of 50 percent while taxing earned income of the $4000 a year non-recipient at only 20 percent? But to lower that 50 percent marginal rate while maintaining even the modest guarantee level of $3,000, for example, would distribute substantial benefits to large numbers of people with incomes over $6,000. The only way out of this unsatisfactory dilemma—terminating benefit eligibility before the $6000 figure—results in an actual *decline* in net take home pay over a certain income range.

THE FAMILY ASSISTANCE PLAN: A SOLUTION?

No better example of a mix of strategies could be found than the efforts of the Nixon administration to put together a workable package of welfare reform. Both pragmatic analysis and political necessity have expanded the original income guarantee scheme advocated by Daniel P. Moynihan to include elements of a children's allowance, work incentives, day care, job training, and fiscal relief for state and local governments. In the process of making the plan politically acceptable the principle of universal guaranteed income has been obscured, especially as it might apply to the working poor

Presented publicly in August 1969 and as draft legislation in October 1969, the original Family Assistance Plan worked through existing state and federal programs to provide a basic federal income guarantee. In essence it could be described as a negative income tax for families with children, guaranteeing $1,600 a year for a family of four. The first $720 of earned income was to be disregarded in benefit calculations, and benefits would be reduced by 50 cents on the dollar beyond that until a total income of $3,920 (for a family of four) was reached.

Applicants for assistance had to submit to a "work test," meaning that they had to register with the U.S. Employment Service and agree to accept work defined as suitable, or accept job training. Failure to do one of these things would result in cutoff of the applicant's aid portion, but not the benefits due the remainder of his family. Incentive payments would be made to trainees, training programs would be expanded, and day care centers would also be expanded to allow mothers to go back to work. Mothers whose children were all of school age would be required to submit to the work test. The food stamp plan was to be coordinated with family assistance so that a family of four could receive total benefits of $2,464 cash equivalent.

This first set of proposals encountered congressional opposition based on the two most powerful arguments in the conservative repertoire—excessive cost and excessive centralism. The House Ways and Means Committee reported the plan favorably in 1970 and it passed the House in April of that year. In the Senate Finance Committee, however, caught between conservative complaints of "too much" and liberal criticisms of "too little," it was delayed until December. The December committee action, coupling family assistance with foreign trade restrictions and Social Security increases, was talked to death by opponents of the trade provisions and critics of the plan's low benefit levels.

In addition to the questions of cost and centralism, FAP's conservative critics were also worried about its work incentive effects. They were obviously concerned that extension of welfare aid would undermine the self-reliance of recipients—the same specter that has always been raised against welfare programs in the United States. Their fears had a clear political significance: the idea of increasing welfare rolls and raising benefit levels at a time of severe inflationary squeeze for the nonwelfare majority, even in the name of welfare reform, is certain to be unpopular; any congressman voting for such a proposal would have to do a lot of unpleasant explaining to his constituents at election time.

The strength of congressional worries about work incentives becomes clearer when placed in the context of informed discussion about welfare reform at the time the original Nixon proposals were being considered. The climate of professional opinion was certainly in favor of an income guarantee, even if public sentiment was uncertain. In November 1969 the President's Commission on Income Maintenance (the Heineman Commission, appointed by President Johnson) submitted a report advocating higher national minimum payment standards ($2,400 for a family of four) and the granting of welfare aid as a matter of right.[5] In February 1970 a preliminary report on a negative income tax experiment conducted by the Office of Economic Opportunity (also begun under President Johnson) generally supported the feasibility of aid payments to working families. It concentrated on the work incentive effects of aid, short circuiting the most extreme fears raised by the concept of guaranteed income.[6] In April 1970 the Committee for Economic Development, an influential business research group, published a report calling for a $2,400 basic guarantee level coupled to some form of work test.[7] Apparently shunting these proposals aside, however, Congress did not find the original Nixon welfare reform plan acceptable.

The new Nixon proposals as they were reported by the House Ways and Means Committee in May 1971 attempt to deal with the specific objections made against the earlier version of the plan. Changes in FAP itself respond to conservative criticisms, while additional features packaged along with FAP appeal to all congressmen, conservative or liberal, through the device of fiscal relief for state and local governments.

The new proposals sidestep the controversy over Food Stamps by declaring cash aid recipients ineligible for them and increasing the basic cash guarantee to $2,400 for a family of four. Families will be required to move off FAP at lower levels of earned income than in the earlier plan ($2,400 as against $3,920) and they will get to keep less of their earned income while under the plan (a marginal tax rate of 67 percent on earned income instead of 50 percent). The first $720 of earned income yearly will still be untaxed.

The most significant addition to the reform package is a new

Opportunities for Families Program. Of the approximately 4 million families to be covered by new components of the package, about 2.6 million would be covered by OFP. Under this program employable adults, including those currently employed at low wages, must register for work or job training. They will benefit in turn from a variety of services in the program—day care, minor medical and transportation expenses, public service jobs, job training and placement, and other manpower services. Trainees will receive a $30 per month incentive payment to remain in training.

Administratively there are now to be two programs instead of one: the OFP administered by the Department of Labor, with its traditional orientation toward improving the position of the working man, and the FAP handled by the Department of Health, Education and Welfare, with its welfare emphasis. The administrative procedure has also been exactly reversed: instead of treating all families as eligible for income support and then applying a work test if there is an employable adult in the family, families will now be presumed candidates for OFP unless they can demonstrate the absence of an employable person in the family. Little more than one family in three is expected to be in FAP. Apparently, though, participation in OFP is supposed to be just a transitional state, since families in OFP will not have a guaranteed income. They will instead get a variety of "in kind" benefits all designed to make gainful employment possible.

Several features of the 1971 welfare reform package have broad political appeal beyond their reform impact. Most important of these are the "hold harmless" clause, which pays the states for any increase in welfare costs over their 1971 levels, and complete federalization of the three federally assisted categories (aside from AFDC): old age assistance, aid to the blind, and aid to the permanently and totally disabled. In addition, for 22 states the new federal minimum is higher than present benefit levels, meaning a probable complete federal takeover of welfare financing for those states.

THE FUTURE OF INCOME MAINTENANCE POLICY

It may be unfair to criticize the Family Assistance Plan on grounds of abstract principle. Nevertheless, to effect any major change in income policy in the face of opposition to the principle of guaranteed income, it has been necessary to compromise that principle nearly to the vanishing point. The FAP itself, with its guarantee features, will still apply only to "deserving" recipients, even though the deserving group has been expanded.

It certainly is unfair to direct all criticism at the Nixon administration, in view of the substantial congressional obstacles to income policy change. Congress, for the most part, is responsible for rewriting the original income guarantee plan as a simple welfare reform and revenue sharing package, and it is in Congress that any further modification of income policy will be tested for political acceptability.

The Opportunities for Families Program is a brave measure, for it proposes to tackle income poverty through the same job-training and job-finding approaches—similar to the Job Corps, for example—that have proved slow and expensive in the past. Attempts to create large numbers of low wage jobs will only worsen the minimum wage policy dilemma: how to keep the statutory minimum wage above the poverty line without pricing labor out of the market. If jobs cannot be found in industry through OFP, federal policy makers will have two choices: they can admit that income support is necessary even for the employable poor, or they can create jobs on the WPA model, through direct governmental hiring. It is hard to imagine Congress liking either of these choices, but if the federal government assumes responsibility for all the poor, through whatever plan, it can hardly drop that responsibility when one plan falls through.

The 1971 welfare reform proposals do chart one clear course for income policy—continuing federalization of state and local aid programs. For welfare reformers it offers a chance to equalize benefit levels among states, for guarantee advocates it offers a large lever for change in the state programs, and for state politicians it grants relief from the political costs of rising state taxes.

Ideologically the centralizing aspects of federal funding may be objectionable to conservatives, but will probably not be as objectionable as its positive features are beneficial. Liberals will continue to push for higher benefits, broader coverage, and less restrictive regulation, while conservatives will attempt to hold down costs and reassert principles of work incentive and individual responsibility. As part of an omnibus reform package, further federalization may be an attractive compromise between these two extremes.

Whether a clear principle of income guarantee will ever be adopted as the foundation of income policy in this country still seems a highly speculative question. Necessity may force a change in the reality of income policy, but not a change in its supposed principles. While the failure of other approaches may open the way for a universal negative income tax scheme, in operation it probably will be sufficiently limited to permit denial of the principle of universal coverage. But at that point principles will be largely irrelevant, because the needed reforms will have been accomplished.

Notes

[1] Mollie Orshansky, "The Shape of Poverty in 1966," *Social Security Bulletin* 31 (March 1968): pp. 3–32.

[2] U.S. Bureau of the Census, *Current Population Reports,* Series P-60, no. 77 (May 7, 1971).

[3] Michael Harrington, *The Other America* (New York: Macmillan, 1962).

[4] *The New York Times,* October 30, 1969, p. 51.

[5] President's Commission on Income Maintenance, *Poverty Amid Plenty: The American Paradox* (Washington, D.C.: U.S. Government Printing Office, 1969).

[6] Office of Economic Oportunity, "Preliminary Results of the New Jersey Graduated Work Incentive Experiment," February 18, 1970.

[7] Committee for Economic Development, *Improving the Public Welfare System* (New York: CED, 1970).

9

Air and Water Pollution

From one point of view, the pollution question has an easy answer. It's a simple matter of good guys and bad guys—"average citizens" and "irresponsible private interests"—engaged in a continuing power struggle over the future of "the environment." For the average citizens to win, the special interests must be defeated, and for that to happen the average citizens must rise up and demand their rights to clean air and clean water. They must mobilize to stiffen the backbone of legislative bodies against corruption by automobile companies, power companies, oil interests, and other powerful and effective pollution lobbies, and they must insist that strict regulations be imposed to stop all pollution immediately.

Most people would accept this simple solution. But if the same basic issues are raised in the guise of "water resources management" or "air quality standards" or sewage treatment costs and rates or power plant cooling devices—the terms in which pragmatic solutions must be discussed—few people will know where they stand. This gap between rhetoric and practical knowledge generates considerable frustration and confusion, making clear analysis of pollution policy almost impossible.

The difficulty with simplistic approaches is the unreliability of their answers. For instance, the current enthusiasm for some kind of electric automobile indicates at best substantial technical ignorance or misinformation. When the efficiency of the overall process of producing electric power needed to charge and recharge the storage batteries in an electric car is compared to the efficiency of the internal combustion gasoline engine, the supposed superiority of the electric car largely evaporates. The real choice becomes not one between greater and lesser degrees of efficiency or pollution, but one between the kinds of pollutants produced now by electric generating plants versus those produced by internal combustion engines, with some consideration given to probable improvements in these two competing technologies.

Antipollution rhetoric also frequently covers up another aspect of the environmental question—the fact that each of us has some detrimental impact on our environment and therefore that each of us must be numbered among the "bad guys." While politics does not always force pollution activists to acknowledge their own guilt, this broader perspective is essential for policy analysis purposes. If the overtones of righteousness are removed from the antipollution argument, it becomes possible to treat pollution policy choices explicitly as questions of relative values, or of costs and benefits associated with different possible solutions. Pollution is basically an economic problem, and only by exploring its economic facets are we likely to resolve it in acceptable fashion.

Suppose that the following headline were to appear in tomorrow's newspaper:

AIR POLLUTION IN LOS ANGELES
AT CRITICAL LEVEL
CITY MAY BAN ALL CARS

The article under this headline describes an emergency situation created by unusually heavy auto traffic and a temperature inversion which is preventing normal dissipation of smog in the Los Angeles area.

This story would surprise very few people. After all, everyone knows that Los Angeles has about the worst air pollution problem in the country, and it therefore must be only a matter of time before a real crisis situation occurs.

Then suppose that the following headline appears the same day on a feature article:

L.A. REPORTS PROGRESS IN SMOG CLEANUP
STRICT ENFORCEMENT PAYS OFF, OFFICIALS SAY

In the article pollution experts praise the ban on backyard incinerators and the auto emission standards for bringing about a substantial reduction in air pollution in Los Angeles, and they predict further improvement as a result of positive state and local action.

This story also would probably not surprise too many people, since the situation in Los Angeles has become so severe that some strong measures obviously are necessary. California, of course, has been in the vanguard of state regulation of automobile exhaust emissions, and it is not surprising that these efforts are beginning to have an effect.

The point of this hypothetical comparison is simply that both articles could be true. Air pollution in Los Angeles has been substantially reduced in the last few years, but there are still smog alerts and children are still kept inside during school recess when the smog is particularly bad.

When a city's pollution record is at the same time "better" and "not good enough" even the most careful examination of the objective data on pollution will not yield much insight. The national figures for pollutants released into the air are 580,000 tons per day, or about 6 pounds per person per day, and this average probably underestimates the extent of pollution in the air over Los Angeles.[1] The bald figure of 6 pounds per person per day is unquestionably pollution. But is it too much pollution? Does it demand, as the first hypothetical article suggests, drastic action to prevent a major disaster? Or does it in fact represent progress and improvement, as the second article says? Can a solution to the Los Angeles problem be delayed five years? At what cost? What does clean air look like, anyway?

While total figures for amounts of pollutants are staggering, they represent only very small percentage concentrations in the atmosphere. On the other side of the argument, though, some of the more noxious pollutants such as carbon monoxide and sulphur oxides are highly dangerous in concentrations less than one part per million.

One of the great stumbling blocks to understanding the pollution problem is the absence of commonly accepted standards for identifying "too much" pollution. Raw figures mean nothing in themselves. No one could honestly say that 580,000 tons of pollutants per day is too much without building an elaborate framework in several disparate sciences, such as meteorology and biology, and trying to relate his observed raw data back to research evidence in these scientific disciplines. Obviously the casual reader or the average city resident is in no position to determine for himself whether there is a pollution problem or not, except in the immediate evidence offered to him by his eyes and nose.

Some environmental activists argue that any amount of pollution is undesirable, especially if it has any significant effect on human life, or even on plant and animal life. On first hearing this point of view appears very attractive, but a little reflection will demonstrate that public policy is never made, and never can be made, on the basis of such absolute standards.

The federal highway program provides a useful comparison. The interstate highway system is relatively safe to travel on, and certainly is much safer than the roads it replaced. But it is also very expensive. Highway safety advocates might argue that the system should be engineered to be absolutely safe, but to do so would make the system so expensive that it would never be built. What happens, instead, is that the Federal Highway Administration sets design standards for the system that imply "reasonable" costs per mile of constructed road, and of course also imply the probability per mile of an accident. In effect, some kind of trade between safety and cost has been made, even if the terms of this trade have never been specifically acknowledged.

Practically speaking, the pollution question must be answered in a similar fashion, through some kind of trade between the amount of pollution reduction the public desires and the amount of money it is willing to commit to pollution control. But pollution does differ from public highways in one important respect. The public roads in the United States have largely been paid for through gasoline taxes, license fees, and tolls, so that their cost is borne by those who benefit directly from the roads. Pollution, on the other hand, can be generated by one person, affect a second, and be abated at the expense of yet a third person or group of people.

It is this characteristic of pollution as a public good that opens up the possibility of political solutions which go beyond the simple economics applied to the construction and maintenance of roads. It is this characteristic of pollution, also, that raises the question of whether, even in an economic sense, polluters should always be required to pay the entire cost of pollution control. In other words, while pollution may possess some features of a simple regulatory problem (category 3 in Chapter 6) it may even more appropriately be seen as a public good (category 5).

Before proceeding to an analysis it may be useful to set down a few of the quantitative dimensions of the problem as it now stands. Except for the impact of municipal storm and sanitary sewers and city water systems, this picture, shown in Tables 16 and 17, is largely a description of the result of unregulated private actions. Direct regulation is sufficiently embryonic that it has little effect, as yet, on gross pollution statistics.

Pollution Economics

WHY DO PEOPLE POLLUTE?

There is no free lunch, economists are fond of saying, but they might add that you can often get someone else to pay the

Table 16
Air Pollution and Its Sources

What is it?	*Millions of tons per year*
Carbon monoxide	100
Sulphur oxides	33
Particulates	28
Nitrogen oxides	21
Miscellaneous	32
Total	214
Who does it?	*Millions of tons per year*
Automobiles	91
Heating and power plants	46
Factories	29
Incinerators and dumps	11
Miscellaneous sources	37
Total	214

Source: National Air Pollution Control Administration estimates, 1970.

Table 17
The Economics of Pollution

Estimated current yearly costs (in billions)		*Estimated yearly abatement costs (five-year average) (in billions)*
$13.5	Air	$2.6
12.0	Water	10.8
—	Solid	0.8
$25.5	Total	$14.2

Source: Figures cited in *U.S. News and World Report* (August 17, 1970), p. 39.

bill for you. Such pragmatic sentiments lie at the heart of the pollution problem, for they describe exactly the approach that any sensible person takes to pollution control.

To make this basic point, consider a very simple situation from which many of the complexities of the real world have been removed. Imagine a society of 100 people, in which each person is inclined to pollute the air, water, and other natural resources to an equal degree. If the cost to each individual to cease his own pollution is taken to be one unit, a plausible total benefit from the cessation of one individual's pollution might also be about one unit. Each person in society would get 1/100 of that total benefit, or about .01 units. Whenever the total social benefit is greater than one unit for each unit cost of cessation, "society" as a whole benefits from cessation. But in this simple society pollution costs are wholly private in nature because they are assumed voluntarily, while benefits are enjoyed equally by all. In short, voluntary pollution abatement in a free-choice society will not take place unless the total benefits of abatement are at least 100 times the cost, an unlikely situation.

Another way to express the same point is to realize that anyone in this model society can enjoy the convenience of a "free" right to pollute by forgoing only 1/100 of the benefits of his own forebearance. The results of this situation are obvious. No one in his right mind would take the burden of pollution control on his own shoulders—it just would not pay. And it wouldn't work, either.

So the society is in a bind. Its 100 members are all acting rationally, and no one could advise them to behave some other way. The problem is not that they want pollution; presumably they don't. The problem is instead that "society" cannot express its preferences directly, but must rely on its individual members to do so. This situation gives rise to a classic problem in welfare economics, because the perspectives of the individual and society at large inevitably differ on the crucial question of costs and benefits of any social action.

To repeat, scarcely any positive action will benefit a single individual as long as its benefits are widely dispersed. What this society needs in short order, if it does not already have one, is a government empowered to coerce all citizens, or a substantial proportion of them, to take antipollution actions that, collectively, will be of benefit to all. Until the narrow self-interested calculations of individuals are changed, little voluntary pollution control will occur. Apparently this is the current state of affairs in the United States, for as Table 17 shows it would be cheaper to control pollution than to let it go unchecked. But the catch is, cheaper for whom? A look at corporate polluters suggests further answers.

WHY DO CORPORATIONS POLLUTE?

The simple answer to this question is, they pollute for the same reasons individuals do. In accounting terms, pollution simply does not exist for most manufacturers. Very few of them reckon up their impact on the environment, because they do not have to. The businessman, going about his business, is primarily concerned with measurable profits and losses. He will respond to the environmental issue only when it begins to have a measurable effect on his profit picture. Normally the manufacturer, while he may produce pollution as a side effect of his enterprise, neither sells it nor is forced to pay for it. Rarely, for example, does he suffer loss of sales because of his pollution record. Consumers generally do not know and do not care to know anything about the manufacturing process by which their purchases are created, and if they do, the relevant information proves very elusive.

Rarely, also, does a given manufacturer's pollution enter into his own costs to any significant extent. If he is a heavy user of water, for example, he simply takes water in upstream and releases it downstream. If he releases large quantities of airborne waste, he builds a high stack to put those pollutants into moving air currents that will carry them away from his factory. If he happens to need large quantities of pure air in his manufacturing process he must filter the air (and of course that will cost something), but air and water filtering, when they are necessary, are merely costs of doing business. For accounting purposes they are treated like any other cost—raw materials or labor, for instance. A manufacturer could himself cease to pollute but that action would not eliminate the need for filtering because many other people contribute to the pollution level he finds at his air intake. In other words, his incentives to cease pollution are no greater than those offered to individuals in the model society analyzed above.

Corporations are different from individuals, however, in that they can often escape paying for pollution even when government regulation is imposed upon them. From the corporate point of view, the value of manufactured goods is determined by the market. It does not directly concern a manufacturer if some of the cost of his production is not reflected in his product's market price but is instead represented by the expense forced on his neighbors by his air and water pollution. So, if for some reason he is forced to clean up his pollution, thus relieving his neighbors of the hidden costs they would otherwise pay, he will naturally try to push the costs of cleanup back on them again rather than paying it himself.

A manufacturer may be able to escape paying in several ways: perhaps by getting tax relief for the pollution control expense he is forced to incur, thus pushing the cost onto taxpayers; perhaps by threatening to take his business and the jobs and income it creates out of the neighborhood unless he gets some economic aid or a special exemption; or perhaps by adding the cost of pollution control to his product's market price, thus forcing his customers to pay. These different responses on the part of the manufacturer may have slightly different effects in terms of who ultimately must bear the cost of the enforced antipollution measures, but from the manufacturer's viewpoint they share one important similarity—someone else foots the bill.

Since most businesses are really only economic middlemen, it is important to recognize that they cannot be made to pay the ultimate costs of pollution control. At best the owners of corporations (stockholders) may be forced to take profit cuts (lower dividends), but whether or not that happens depends on the economic market and not on governmental policy.

Some manufacturers have jumped on the environmental bandwagon, avidly promoting antipollution products and trying to sell a new corporate image of "pollution fighter" to the public at large. Again, though, the basic motivation for this flurry of ecological consciousness is not ecological concern per se, but profit and the prospects for profit. While this is probably as it should be, it can produce some strange and amusing results. For instance, a spokesman for the Monsanto company, appearing before a Senate subcommittee in 1969, testified that he had not succeeded in selling one of the company's new antipollution products to the Monsanto company itself, although he admitted reluctantly that the company could certainly use the product.[2]

And this company is far from being the only such case. The reason for this seemingly incongruous behavior is obvious: the new products division thinks it can make a profit selling antipollution equipment, while the operating division thinks it can save money by continuing to pollute. The company's right hand may not appear to know what its left hand is doing, but even if it did, company policy would be the same.

Two Partial Solutions

REGULATION OF LOCAL NEIGHBORHOOD EFFECTS

Presuming that the control of pollution is still a major policy goal, even if polluters cannot always be made to pay for it, there are some circumstances in which policy guidelines can be set down. The first example represents a somewhat special case, for it assumes that individual polluters and individual victims can be identified, and furthermore that direct connections can be established between these two groups. Pollution control according to this model is carried out against a background provided by the larger pollution problem since most pollution probably cannot be so easily identified.

Typical of this situation is the backyard leaf burner. If everyone burns leaves in the fall, then any single individual is safe from the censure of his neighbors. But if no one burns leaves, then any single offender can easily be identified as a public nuisance, and appropriate action can be taken against him. Common law, for instance, recognizes such cases and provides legal recourse against such persons on the grounds that they and their actions are impairing the rights of free use and enjoyment of property on the part of the nonpolluting neighbor.

But a lawyer from the back of the room may say, "That's not policy at all, that's law." Someone else may say, "That really has nothing to do with pollution. Pollution is something far more important and widespread than any solution that relies on finding and prosecuting nuisances."

Several points can be made in reply to these criticisms. First, the extent of disturbance to society is not at issue here, but simply the extent of damage done by any individual polluter to any individual nonpolluter. The impact of any individual industrial polluter may not be great when spread across the country, for example, but the chances are that its impact is much more concentrated in some places than others. Neighbors to a factory would not be impressed that it produces only a fraction of a percent of total pollution if at the same time it produces half of the pollution *they* suffer. They know where their pollution problem is, and they know what to do about it. The collective effect of hundreds of such actions across the country should not be underestimated either.

A second reply to the critics of this legal approach is that such a strategy need not rely solely on private initiative in bringing complaints and initiating legal action. Governmental units can be granted the power to take up the cudgel for private individuals as long as the basic conditions are met: the number and general location of the victims must be clearly identified and the sources of pollution must also be identifiable. In fact, since discretionary governmental regulation opens up the question of equitable treatment of those being regulated, such regulation tends to expand to all areas of pollution because of the logic of the regulatory argument.

When a governmental body, federal, state, or local, becomes involved in this way it adopts the familiar "public health" approach under which governmental initiative has been justified for so long that public responsibility is essentially taken for granted. At a very mundane level, for example, cities have provided sewers and city garbage collection for a long time under this general public health rubric. Aside from questions of equity, it is not much more controversial to regulate pollution on the same basis.

NEIGHBORHOOD EFFECTS: WHO PAYS?

Once governmental regulatory authority is extended into an industry, a whole range of questions about costs and burdens comes into view. The basic question is, who ultimately pays for regulation? While it is hopelessly naive to assume that the immediate targets of regulation will foot the entire bill, it is by no means easy to determine exactly who will pay. Pollution regulators themselves are not greatly concerned about this kind of question since their goal is to reduce pollution to an acceptably low level, not to make a profit for a producer or to keep a consumer's prices low. The regulated producer, however, and the consumer of his products, will be very interested in these matters because it is their profits and costs that are being directly affected.

Most, but not all, the escape hatches available to a producer depend strongly on the economics of his position in his industry and in the market for his products. One solution that is not so constrained is for the company to seek local assistance in meeting the cost of antipollution equipment. How successful the company is in this strategy depends more critically on political factors than on economic ones, since the essence of the strategy is bargaining. For this "blackmail" strategy to be at all effective, the company attempting it must have an important place in its local economy. This may be the case even for a company which has a very small share of the national market for its product or for a company which is not particularly profitable to operate. All that is necessary is for the company to confer substantial benefits on its place of location through providing jobs and income. When regulation is suggested, the company asserts that it may have to leave the community if regulatory standards are imposed because it could not meet the standards and still be economical to operate.

A situation similar to the outline above occurred recently in Duluth, Minnesota. There a plant of the U.S. Steel Corporation was, after a long series of conferences, put under orders by the state's Pollution Control Agency to meet state clean air standards by a given date or begin to pay fines and possibly other penalties as well. U.S. Steel claimed that the plant was one of the least profitable owned by the company, that it was relatively old, and that the company could not make the financial investment required to meet the pollution standards.

The citizens of Duluth responded with alarm to the company's threat that they might shut down the plant rather than comply with the standards, since the plant was a major employer in the city and the overall economic situation in the city was not good. If the plant stayed it would continue to pollute the air of Duluth, but it would also continue to employ many thousands of workers who had no other prospects for employment in the city. If the plant were shut down the air would be clearer but many workmen would face extended unemployment.

In this situation the city chose neither pollution nor unemployment, instead committing itself to find sources of funds for the necessary antipollution equipment. Whether this proposal could be put into effect was very much an open question at the time it was made, but U.S. Steel at least came out of the whole episode in good position: they had been granted some additional time to comply with the air quality standards.

In effect, U.S. Steel was bluffing. They claimed that the Duluth plant was uneconomical to operate, but no one outside U.S. Steel could really confirm or deny that statement. In addition, no one outside the company could have second-guessed the action that the managers of the parent corporation would take if faced with "impossible" pollution standards at one of their plants. There was some skepticism that the plant would actually be shut down, but very few people could afford to call the company's bluff by taking no action. Thus the company did manage to shift some of its costs onto someone else.

Most companies cannot "hold up" a city to get special treatment or special help in paying for pollution control equipment because they are not big enough to represent a sizable chunk of the city economy. For such companies, the impact of antipollution regulation will be determined solely by the economic position of the company in the industry and in the market, and the answers to the question "What will happen?" are almost as varied as the industries.

The National Air Pollution Control Administration (NAPCA) published some careful pollution cost estimates for four industries in early 1970. These four industries are all high air polluters, so the cost figures may be somewhat extreme, but the study does point out the wide range of possible economic effects. Table 18 shows the estimated cost data for each of the industries in the study.[3] How these costs are distributed depends, NAPCA concluded, on the market structure in each industry. Gray iron foundries, for instance, typically are small local establishments, generally operating in a competitive environment. NAPCA estimated that the average cost increase of 10 percent for the foundries would drive many of them out of business unless their local competitive position allowed them to pass a substantial portion of that cost on to their customers.

The Kraft process pulp manufacturers, while officially separate manufacturing operations, are nearly all integrated with paper

Table 18
Estimated "Clean Air" Costs for Four High-Pollution Industries

	Initial cost (in millions)	*Annual cost (in millions)*
Gray iron foundries	$305	$ 92
Kraft paper pulp	86	35
Iron and steel		
Boilers	3	17
Sintering	88	33
Steelmaking	466	178
Steam electric power		
Boilers	252	39
Particulates and SO_2	953–1,403	319–616

Source: National Air Pollution Control Administration estimates, 1970.

manufacturers and economically subservient to them. Hence paper makers, according to NAPCA, would resist any attempted price increase that the pulp manufacturers might use to cover pollution control expenses, and the end result would be an 8–10 percent drop in net income after taxes for the pulp makers.

Iron and steel makers, on the other hand, are relatively few in number and generally operate on the basis of administered prices. Foreign competition would be an important factor in when and how much prices were increased to cover pollution control in basic iron and steel. One noteworthy effect of control in this industry, NAPCA said, would be the wide diffusion of cost increases into other industries since iron and steel are such basic items.

Steam electric power, finally, shows somewhat different results depending on how much cleanup is attempted. Emissions from boilers could be controlled at a cost low enough that it could be absorbed, passed backward to coal suppliers, or broadly dispersed through small rate increases. Control of sulphur oxides would be sufficiently costly that rate increases would be needed, assuming emission standards equivalent to the use of coal of only 1 percent sulphur content. These standards could be met by substituting other fuels for coal, but NAPCA quickly pointed out that substitution of this kind would have serious economic impacts on the coal and rail industries which are both strongly tied up with power companies.

COMMON POOL RESOURCES

One of the peculiaries that restricts the kinds of solutions possible for air pollution problems is the obvious fact that air pollution cannot be treated once it gets into the air. Regulators must rely, then, on identifying pollution sources and controlling pollution at the source.

This limitation does not apply to water pollution. Virtually everywhere in the United States water is delivered to the industrial or private user through a municipal water system. Storm and sanitary sewage is collected and treated at a common point by the municipal water system. Water, in other words, is a "common pool resource," which everyone to greater or lesser extent pollutes and also benefits from.

For reasons of convenience and economy of scale, it is most common for water treatment to be handled through some central governmental agency. Provision of adequate clean water is thus viewed as a public good to be supported through some kind of compulsory taxing mechanism, since voluntary action by individual users of the resource cannot be counted on to do enough to maintain it.

The problem with common pool resources that necessitates their treatment as public goods is basically a problem of costs, but simply "nationalizing" such resources through public management does not solve the costs problem. On the contrary, questions of cost become all important when governmental decision makers must set priorities among different classes of users, to decide the relative merits of different kinds of costs, and generally to apportion the total cost burden of water supply among those who benefit from it.

Water pollution control through municipal or regional sewer and water systems is largely a matter of public finance. Therefore, where these systems are not supported by some larger source of tax revenue such as a sales or general property tax they must be maintained by a set of special charges. Levying these charges breaks down logically into two separate problems: (1) allocating charges between users and nonusers of the system and (2) allocating charges among categories of system users.

Distribution of costs between users and nonusers can be made in many ways. The great number of theories precludes any detailed summary, but it is important to note how wide the range of plausible results is. First, though, we should insert a note about the economists' notion of a "nonuser." Virtually everyone uses the sewerage system, but some people derive benefits from that system beyond direct use-related benefits. Property owners, for example, find their property worth more when it is well drained of storm water, and nearly everyone benefits from the lower likelihood of disease associated with efficient sewerage. The differing theories of cost allocation rest on differing assumptions about the relative importance of these additional nonuser benefits.

If it is assumed that combined storm and sanitary sewers are operated essentially for reasons of public convenience and efficiency, then the sewerage system is treated as a public utility, similar to postal service, and is financed entirely out of user charges. Individuals who pollute pay the full cost of their polluting activity. At the other extreme, if it is assumed that benefits from storm and sanitary sewers are diffused widely among users and nonusers, then it is logical to supply these sewers out of general revenues provided by taxing both users and nonusers. In this view individual acts of pollution are not penalized; if anything, there is a popular belief that pollution is a kind of "right" that everyone can enjoy.

Between these extremes a variety of theories have been proposed, depending to varying degrees on the possession of precise knowledge regarding the sources, amounts and kinds of sewage being processed at any moment. Perhaps the simplest of these middle-ground approaches assumes that the costs in a combined system can be divided between the storm drainage functions and the sanitary sewerage functions. Then the storm drainage costs are allocated among nonusers and the additional costs necessary to provide sanitary sewerage in the same system are apportioned among users. Another simple, but arbitrary theory asserts that capital costs should be carried by property owners (nonusers) since the system is built so as to connect various parcels of property to the system, and the remaining operating and maintenance costs should be paid by users because these costs are incurred as a result of use of the system.

The Federal Water Quality Administration (FWQA) examined these same issues in its 1970 report, "The Economics of Clean Water" but it shied away from making specific recommendations to localities other than to suggest some division of cost between users and nonusers, with a larger proportion of operating

Table 19
Evaluation of Three Water User Charge Plans

Criterion	*Flat rate*	*Volume rate*	*Biochemical oxygen demand*
Equity	Worst	Good	Best
Efficiency	Worst	Fair	Best
Ease of administration	Best	Good	Worst
Revenue adequacy	Worst	Best	Good

costs being carried by users. One obvious reason for the FWQA's reluctance is to be found in the widely varying local use pictures, depending in turn on widely varying local rainfall, supply costs, and the like. Another probable reason for the absence of specific recommendations is that inevitably allocations and rate decisions are made by a process that is highly political, and for which economic guidelines may not be very useful.

But even after nonusers have been charged, the ratesetter still has substantial latitude in dividing costs among users on a purely economic basis. He may adopt any one of a number of bases on which rates may be calculated, or he may choose a combination of them. The most common elements in user charges for sewerage are a flat or minimum rate, a volume rate, and a rate based on "biochemical oxygen demand" (BOD) or on some other specific chemical characteristic of the discharged waste. Individually, no one of these components of the total charge is clearly superior to the others across the board, although each is superior in some respect. Table 19 roughly indicates how these components rank on four standard criteria often applied to tax systems. Obviously when cities formulate a combined rate system they are putting together some kind of compromise suited to the particular kinds of users and treatment prevailing in that city.

One method that almost certainly will *not* be used is calculation of the exact cost incurred in supplying each individual user. While this approach would be the fairest economically, it does not in fact pay the city water service to calculate charges to the last penny because administration itself costs money. Most sys-

Table 20
Distribution of User Charge Burden for Sewerage under Different Formulas*

Type of user	*Flat rate*	*Volume*	*BOD load*	*Property value*
Residential	94.2%	59.5%	45.7%	69.8%
Commercial	5.3	9.2	12.3	22.2
Industrial	0.4	27.4	36.7	8.0
Other	0.1	3.9	5.2	0.0
Total	100.0%	100.0%	100.0%	100.0%

Source: Federal Water Pollution Control Agency, *The Cost of Clean Water and Its Economic Impact* (1969), Vol. III, p. 54.

* Data are illustrative, estimated for a "typical" large city.

tems content themselves with choosing among a relatively small number of types of charge systems, perhaps introducing some explicit sliding scales, and sticking with their choice.

A more important reason why the "obvious" exact cost method is not used in rate setting is that some rate structures may have (intentional) redistributive effects. The provision of even so mundane a service as sewerage, because it is provided publicly, becomes a possible source of subsidy benefits for some users at the expense of others, or at the expense of nonusers. Sewerage is a valuable service, especially if the alternative is that individuals would be legally required to provide sanitary substitutes, and to the extent that some users get more for their money than others, some subsidization is taking place.

Now it could be the case that public water and sewer service is so efficient when compared to private alternatives that everyone would find the public system to be the cheapest alternative. In that case everyone benefits, of course, but some could still benefit more than others and could thus be enjoying a kind of "relative subsidy." But the basic rate schemes produce such markedly different distributions of cost, as Table 20 shows, that most real systems undoubtedly do generate subsidy benefits of substantial size.

One brief lesson should be obvious from the discussion so far: you can't escape politics. An analyst approaching pollution from an economic point of view quickly discovers that there is plenty of room for politics to influence the solution to seemingly economic problems, either because economics does not dictate the complete terms of the solution or because political forces may override economic values when public decisions are made. For example, in water service rate setting, the choice among alternate rate schemes—or even the specific details of rate structures—may be consciously biased to favor one class of user at the expense of another. Furthermore, these biases may have public justifications much the same as other forms of governmental subsidy.

In some cities commercial and industrial users pay an overtly lower rate than residential users for equivalent amounts of service, this subsidy being justified because it supposedly encourages business and industry to locate in the city and remain there, thereby swelling the property tax rolls. For example, the decisions of one large midwestern city in 1970 could be reconstructed as follows:

> We owe the Metropolitan Sewer Board about $7 million for 1970. The current rate structure will not bring in more than about $4 million, but the taxpayers will probably accept a 4 mill increase in the property tax, and that 4 mills would give us another $2 million. With some minor changes in the rate structure we should be able to pay the whole $7 million. Now the Chamber of Commerce has been telling us that the property tax squeeze has hit a lot of businesses hard, and raising the sewer charges might send some of them out of town. If we increase the volume charges but at the same time graduate them, most small businesses will end up paying less. Homeowners will pay more, but we can tell them that the new rates will improve business conditions in the city and may save their jobs.

This kind of effect can occur primarily because there is little areawide rate setting, and individual cities vary considerably in the rates they set for equivalent services. In fact, it is probably the worst polluters who respond most strongly to this rate differential because they stand to gain the most.

While it is true that new industrial plants, and to some extent older plants as well, tend to gravitate to locations where their sewerage charges will be lower, this migration would not produce a serious pollution problem if each local rate were at least adequate to cover minimum necessary treatment costs. Pollution problems do arise, however, because many local units impose inadequate standards or attempt to encourage industry, therefore setting charges which considerably undervalue the social costs of waste and waste treatment.

One of the most useful federal responses to this aspect of the water pollution problem has been the encouragement of regional or watershed conferences and agreements among states for the purpose of setting an areawide water quality standard. To be effective the federal government need not set its own standards and then impose them on separate watershed areas. It may choose instead, as it has done, to urge regional groups to meet and adopt their own standards. The usual means of encouragement is the promise of federal financial support for cooperation, sometimes combined with the threat of unilateral federal action if a regional group fails to produce a set of standards by a certain date.

While this procedure may not eliminate water pollution entirely, it does eliminate some of the more serious inequalities among local regulations. Surveys of local experience demonstrate that corporate polluters do "clean up" when faced with a stiffening of standards—change from a volume rate to a BOD rate, for example—so this simple step can be expected to have positive results.

Pollution and National Politics

THE PUBLIC PERSPECTIVE

In the last few years pollution has sprung into prominence as a major public issue, overshadowing or rivaling crime, the economy, and even Southeast Asia as a source of political interest and a rallying point for citizen activism. As a public issue pollution is nearly ideal—everyone feels the effects of pollution, no one is for it, and everyone can take some part in its solution.

The potency of the environmental appeal can be easily seen, if specific evidence is needed, in the reactions of consumer goods manufacturers. The much heralded availability of unleaded gasoline, for instance, become reality in 1970 only after years of desultory public debate about the effects of leaded gasoline, although the actual changeover of service station facilities took only a few months. The emergence of phosphate-free detergents and the shift of many leading detergent companies to low phosphate formulas also shows the market power of the antipollution movement, as does the spate of popular books on this subject.

Ironically, the rapid rise to prominence of antipollution does not reflect a correspondingly rapid rise in actual pollution. True, also, environmental critics have been around for a long time. But the developments of the last few years in this area are much more clearly an example of the dynamics of political issues than the signs of the emergence of a really new problem. Correspondingly, the emergence of pollution policy should be more closely predicdictable from a study of pollution politics than from a study of the technical aspects of pollution itself. For these reasons the following discussion of pollution politics contrasts markedly with the more strictly economic approach of the first part of this chapter.

Politically, what has happened is that a large number of people have reached a kind of breaking point on pollution and have begun to take action. Their reasons and their immediate impetus to action vary quite a bit, from a polluted lake to a neighbor's pile of burning trash, but together they reinforce each other and encourage further citizen activism. All over the country, people are discovering some basic economic realities. They are discovering that they are not isolated from other people, from animal and plant life, and from their posterity, and this discovery is being converted into a willingness to take action.

Politicians have rushed to meet the demand with new programs and proposals, old environmental watchdogs have found their ranks swelled with new converts, and old line pollution agencies have felt a new and not entirely favorable scrutiny from all sides. Whether this flurry of activity will produce much lasting effect is still largely an unanswered question. As far as public policy is concerned, the source of lasting programmatic changes is still a bureaucratic one, and bureaucracies function quite differently when they slip from the momentary spotlight into the kind of public obscurity they usually experience.

THE REGULATORY JUMBLE

The environmental activist, when he wants action, must first decide where in the labyrinthine pollution bureaucracy he should go. What to the public eye is "the environmental program" is actually little more than an assemblage of separate promotional, licensing, and regulatory actions, each with its own agency, goals, and interest groups. It is only under the pressure of concentrated public attention, such as the United States has seen in the past few years, that any attempt to rationalize these distinct elements into a coherent program can begin.

The Environmental Protection Agency, established by President Nixon in 1970, is such an attempt at coordination, but its existence does not in itself eliminate the continuing problem of policy consistency. The component bureaus and programs of EPA still retain substantial autonomy in budget and personnel matters.

In itself, the fact that pollution policy is made and administered by an elaborate bureaucracy is not fatal as long as this bureaucracy is actually interested in carrying out the directives given to it by Congress or the President. But the problem in American pollution policy is more than simply a cumbersome bureaucracy. The problem is that the bureaucracy holds some exceptionally strong biases in favor of the status quo—that is, in favor of some of the most important sources of pollution.

Of course no one is consciously in favor of pollution per se. But, as discussed in Chapter 4, private holders of economic power can often succeed in getting favorable governmental treatment, either through friendly regulation or through subsidies. In the area of pollution and environmental protection, the impact of regulation and subsidy has been, on the whole, to produce very few changes away from unfettered pollution and toward environmental responsibility.

The critical feature of this process, to review points made in earlier chapters, is that the regulatory bureaucracy comes to depend on the regulated private interests for information and political support. Thus when an attack is made against a private source of pollution, either from outside the government or from a new governmental antipollution agency, the source itself and its supporters in the bureaucracy will come to its defense. Immediately, then, the antipollution battle is loaded with a burden of side issues having to do with the survival of agencies and sometimes the prestige of congressional committees.

At the federal level these policy issues have been clearest in air pollution. Water pollution has suffered less from this kind of politicking because state and local agencies have long been active in this area and water purification and supply has long been a local government function. Thus the major battles in water pollution occur at lower levels in the American federal structure and probably on the whole are more directly legislative than bureaucratic. Most cities and states lack the elaborate bureaucracies that exist at the national level, hence interest groups concerned about water pollution standards must speak directly to legislators in order to have much impact on policy locally.

In air pollution there are no suppliers, of course, and no purifiers. Air and airborne pollutants are by nature more unruly than waterborne pollution, not restricting themselves to channels and not being concentrated enough to be economically treatable by any direct means. The interstate nature of air pollution has severely inhibited the success of any localized attempts at its control and has thus pushed the issue up to the federal level. In addition, until very recently very few people were concerned about the declining quality of air. Federal aid was sought when the emergency character of air pollution was realized and the process of getting action out of each city and state agency seemed much too slow a course.

Another reason for differences between national air and water pollution policies springs from differences in sources of pollution. In water, most of the problem is produced by private home users of water, or by industrial users who dispose of some of the waste products of their production processes in waterways. In air, however, pollution is in large measure caused by industries; in virtually all cases, whether individual or corporate, it is the result of inefficient conversion of energy from one form to another. This is a useful distinction because there is a long history of federal regulation of the energy industry, including production, transportation, transformation, and consumption. At each step along the line, federal policy has had important effects on pollution even though regulation was aimed at energy and not at its principal waste by-products.

This situation is shown clearly by the division of responsibilities among the federal agencies involved with pollution problems: of the forty such agencies in 1970, at least 18 had some connection with energy or fuels policy and thereby some indirect impact on environmental quality in the United States.[4]

PROMOTION, RESEARCH, AND FUEL POLICIES

The fact that an agency makes policy decisions that have an impact on pollution does not make that agency automatically an antipollution agency, nor does it necessarily mean that policy problems in that agency will be viewed as pollution problems. In fact, most of the federal agencies that fall within the compass of pollution policy because of their involvement with energy generation, transmission or sale, persist in seeing their primary tasks as energy regulation rather than pollution control. At best they substantially discount the importance of pollution arguments; at worst they tend to view such criticisms as indirect attacks on their own bureaucratic competence.

Several of the older bureaucratic institutions whose orientation is primarily promotional are housed in the Department of the Interior. The Office of Minerals and Solid Fuels (1962), the Office of Oil and Gas (1946), and the Office of Coal Research (1960) all promote their respective clients in one way or another. The first two agencies are responsible by statute for emergency planning and stockpiling of their respective commodities, and the Office of Coal Research is specifically directed to further efficient coal production and utilization in any way possible.

The Interior Department also includes three power agencies, the Bonneville Power Administration, the Southeastern Power Administration, and the Southwestern Power Administration. These, along with the Tennessee Valley Authority, an independent agency in the executive branch, are empowered to sell "surplus" electric power generated in connection with the federal flood control dams throughout the United States. The dams themselves serve the purpose of natural resource conservation, but at the same time each of these agencies is explicitly directed to sell its power in such a way as to distribute its use most widely and to contribute most significantly to the economic development of the regions in question.

The Atomic Energy Commission finds itself in somewhat similar position with regard to its infant industry. When the decision was made to allow private uses of nuclear power in the United States, the AEC was given the job of promoting the most rapid possible expansion of nuclear power, especially for purposes of power generation. The standard criticism of the AEC, to which it is most sensitive, is that it cannot do a good job of regulating while simultaneously promoting. Thus critics of the AEC's atomic fuel safety claim that the AEC is lax in its standards because it wishes to encourage atomic power generation.

A more sweeping criticism of the AEC's position is simply that its concern for promotion undercuts its responsiveness to any other kind of approach toward electric power generated through atomic energy. Pollution concerns are simply the latest kind of criticism raised against the AEC.

Some of the foregoing agencies, if viewed from the standpoint of pollution policy, seem to be built around internal contradictions. The power administrations, for example, and the AEC, aim to preserve natural resources or protect lives, but at the same time they encourage further power consumption which must surely have some negative effects, either directly or through the by-products of electrical energy production. But even more important, every one of these agencies, whether or not they pursue an internally consistent policy, makes policy decisions that are in part contradictory to the general efforts of other federal agencies to cut back on air and water pollution. By now this is a familiar story, of which the energy regulatory agencies provide only one illustration.

The most common explanation of this phenomenon is that policies develop at different times and for a variety of different reasons. If in the 1960s the energy problem was generally viewed as a problem of imminent shortage while in the 1970s energy itself is seen as a source of environmental problems, then some conflict will almost certainly emerge between agencies and policies of the 1960s and their counterparts in the 1970s.

While this explanation is basically correct, the easy conclusion that energy policy could be rationalized simply by reviewing and revising all existing policy at a single point in time does not really follow. Problems arise because both pollution critics and energy producers have legitimate concerns that must somehow find a place in public policy. Where these interests conflict, some form of compromise must be worked out—it doesn't work to say simply "The consumer is always right" or "What's good for the oil companies is good for the country." For this reason political processes can and inevitably will be invoked to reach final anti-pollution policies. Even if a sweeping review of existing energy policy takes place, the extent of actual policy change will be limited by the political power exerted on behalf of the energy producer interests.

Supposedly, Congress oversees agency operations. But in the course of their promotional activities, regulatory agencies often develop alliances with the parallel substantive congressional committees. The result is virtual atrophy of congressional oversight since the agency and the committee often see themselves allied against outsiders who do not "understand" the complexities of the subject matter of regulation. In the energy regulation field this process almost entirely closes legislative access for the antipollution viewpoint on energy policy.

The relationship between the Atomic Energy Commission and the Joint Committee on Atomic Energy (JCAE), for example, shows this pattern clearly. Early in 1970 this committee released a report more than 1,000 pages long entitled "Environmental Effects of Producing Electric Power." While the length and the title seem to imply great committee concern for environmental and pollution questions, both are partly misleading. The length of the report is explained by the simple fact that it is almost exclusively the transcript of hearings held by the committee in 1969 and materials submitted for the record during those hearings. The report's title is also misleading in that the report is largely a comparison and defense of atomic power against other means of power production, and also a series of friendly exchanges between the committee and witnesses critical of pollution activists and full of praise for the "responsible" viewpoint of federal agencies. The overall impression, in short, is of an event staged largely "for the record."

A few selected sections of the hearings may give some of its flavor. In his opening remarks committee chairman Chet Holifield (D., California) clearly set the stage by stating his own view of the committee's task: "The JCAE's responsibility is to encourage the development of nuclear electric generating plants." [5] In a later exchange with the President's science adviser Lee Dubridge, Holifield stated his own position with regard to environmental critics:

DuBridge: . . . an abundant supply of low cost energy is the key ingredient in continuing to improve the quality of our total environment.

Holifield: In other words, those zealots who propose going on without electrical energy or without increasing electrical energy are not speaking for you or for most of the people in this country.[6]

Later in the hearings a similar point was discussed between Holifield and James T. Ramey, a commissioner for the Atomic Energy Commission. Ramey is cataloguing some of the less helpful lobbyists in the energy field:

Ramey: [First there are] gentlemen from some 'paper' conservation organization that you can hardly find an address for, to persons associated with the coal industry who always seem to be around these days. Second, there is a group of younger scientists, some of whom might be a little bit on the extremist side, who seem to always be talking on matters beyond their own professional competence. . . .

Holifield: But we must not forget that there are some competent people from some of the universities . . . We are going to have people before this committee that do have responsible concerns.

Ramey: That is right. I was going to get to that.[7]

Of course these men and the many others about whom similar statements could be made are entirely sincere in their sentiments about energy and pollution problems. The point is not that they are two-faced; they are not. The point is that close similarities of belief develop between operating agencies and congressional committees, and that contact between agencies and committees in this setting serves primarily to reinforce the biases in existing energy policy.

There is another important link between industries and agencies, and in turn between agencies and Congress—the information and research data link. Much of the information about the energy industry comes from the industry itself since it is essentially information about industry abilities, discoveries, profits and losses, and the like. Information not directly provided by industrial sources is produced by, and more importantly interpreted by, regulatory agencies or promotional bureaus close to industrial interests.

There is at least a suspicion, for instance, that reported shortages of natural gas (a low pollution fuel) may not be as serious as gas industry sources indicate. The point is that no one knows except the gas industry members, and they have never given out information about the exact location of reserves. Sudden drops in the rate of addition to proved reserves can also be interpreted as having political rather than technical causes, but again nobody but the industry knows for sure.

Information about coal reserves provides another illustration. Here the basic data come from the U.S. Geological Survey rather than from industry spokesmen, but the prevailing interpretation is that propagated by the coal industry and coal spokesmen in the Interior Department such as the Bureau of Mines and the Office of Coal Research. The basic findings, which everyone accepts, state that only 10 percent of the nation's low sulphur coal reserves are located east of the Mississippi River. The industry and Interior Department interpretation has been that this is too low an amount to justify a ban on high sulphur coal. This position has also been taken by the Office of Science and Technology in a report entitled, "Considerations Affecting Steam Power Plant Site Selection," sponsored by the Office's Energy Policy Staff and published in late 1968. The OST report bolsters the "inadequate reserves" conclusion with additional industry and agency arguments to the effect that the existing eastern low sulphur coal is largely committed to the steel industry and also serves as an important export commodity, aiding our balance of payments situation.

The OST report, a lengthy well-illustrated document, gives the impression of careful and independent weighing of the evidence, but it is more probable that the OST staff merely compiled the existing conclusions of other agencies. In any case, since the report was written "in cooperation with" the AEC, HEW, Interior, FPC, REA, and TVA, its conclusions must have been considerably influenced by existing agency positions.

The point of this example is simply that the low coal reserves are treated in all the available official documents as an obvious fact. The commitment of our high quality coal to domestic and foreign steel makers is similarly presented as inevitable, and the 10 percent figure is treated as obviously inadequate. But this conclusion, repeated for so long by agency spokesmen, is at least worth examining again. The 10 percent figure represents, on an average estimate, a fifty year supply of high quality coal for the Eastern United States. In the technology of energy production, fifty years would buy a lot of progress.[8]

THE AGENCIES AND PRESSURE POLITICS: WATER

The current status of federal policy for water pollution is relatively limited owing to the feasibility and tradition of local efforts in this area. Basically, the federal government funds local sewerage construction and encourages areawide cooperation on standard setting and on enforcement among existing agencies. As far as explicit antipollution action is concerned, federal policy extends back only to 1948, when the Water Pollution Control Act established an office in the Public Health Service to collect and disseminate information about water pollution and set up a limited abatement procedure the federal government could initiate with the consent of the states involved.

The 1948 policy was modified in 1956 to specify more clearly the necessary time intervals for the various steps in abatement and to change the abatement procedures to require approval only from the state being directly affected by interstate pollution. In addition, the 1956 act established a program of matching grants (30 percent federal, 70 percent local) for sewage treatment plants with an individual project limit of $250,000.

In 1961 the new Kennedy administration increased the amounts authorized under this program and successfully pushed for amendment of the federal abatement powers to include intrastate pollution control, with the state's permission. In the Water Quality Act of 1965 the ceiling on individual construction grants was raised to $1.2 million and the total authorization was raised. In addition, the act required states to set up quality standards acceptable to HEW and it gave the Federal Water Pollution Control Agency independent organizational status in HEW, removing it from the Public Health Service. In 1966 the Clean Water Restoration Act again raised the total authorized amount for matching grants and it eliminated the dollar ceiling on individual grants.

The regular incremental growth of federal involvement in water pollution should not be interpreted as a sign that these changes have been routine or without political controversy. At each step resistance has been expressed, and the outcomes described above are often compromises rather than complete victories for the antipollution forces. During the early years the general ideological issues of federal control versus local responsibility were brought up against federal involvement. Throughout the period from 1948 to the present, industry lobbies such as the Pulp and Paper Manufacturers Association, the U.S. Chamber of Commerce and the National Association of Manufacturers complained that standard setting would work economical hardships on their members, and that the abatement procedures were arbitrary, overly harsh, and too hurried to allow industry a real chance to police itself.

The impact of these lobbying efforts and partisan pressures has been considerable. They have forced caution and forbearance on the FWQA, shifting that agency's attention away from enforcement and toward the less controversial grant-in-aid aspects of federal involvement. Grants-in-aid never hurt anybody, for they neither assign blame nor require correction of undesirable practices. Indeed, by creating the presumption that local sewage systems can keep up with the pollution loads generated by business and individual users, grants shift the focus of problem solution from polluters to pollution treaters. Water pollution becomes almost a matter of unquestioned right.

Table 21
Federal Water Quality Administration Budget, 1970

Programs	*Amount (in millions)*
Research, development, and demonstration	$49
Planning, assistance, and training	39
Executive direction	5
Enforcement	4
Total	$97

Source: Budget for Fiscal Year 1970, Appendix p. 641.

The general "go-slow" approach to pollution abatement forced upon the FWQA by the unwillingness of Congress, and the business and industry interests represented in Congress, to allow swifter action has greatly curtailed federal water pollution activism. In this area, as in other areas of federal regulation—fair employment, for one example—a lengthy series of steps is required, beginning with conferences, then public hearings, and finally court action, with the result that very few enforcement actions are actually completed.

However effective conferring and persuading may be, their usefulness in obstinate cases will certainly be limited unless they carry the clear threat of further action should verbal measures fail. In this regard the FWQA is handicapped in dealing with polluters, but its handicap may be only temporary. With so few complete cases to rely on, both agency and industry representatives look upon each new case as a possible major precedent. A few significant successes by the FWQA, or by the Justice Department, could quickly alter industry expectations and give substantial encouragement to local and state agencies as well.

The biases in federal water pollution policy show clearly in the budget of the FWQA. In 1970, for example, the overwhelming portion of expenses was slated for grant programs, followed by research. Enforcement was a distant third among the agency's major action orientations (see Table 21). The enforcement expenditure level represents only a handful of cases—less than 100 by 1970—and is as yet only a small beginning.

THE AGENCIES AND PRESSURE POLITICS: AIR

Air pollution policy at the federal level displays many of the characteristics ascribed to water pollution policy, but in exaggerated form. In air pollution, the potential federal role is much greater, but so also is the political resistance to federal expansion. The familiar partisan political arguments against federal involvement appear here, and so also do interest group arguments against regulation, clothed in the ideological garb of "local initiative" "decentralization," or "self-help."

Most important, the same kinds of "advisory" interest groups exist in air pollution as in other policy areas, including water pollution. Their effect here is even greater than in other areas because the federal government is exercising almost exclusive control over air pollution regulation and its decisions can be more clearly the target of influence attempts than in other areas of shared state-federal responsibility.

On questions of air quality the businesses who stand behind the present implicit fuels policy and who benefit from its continuance have formed themselves into a variety of industry spokesmen's groups to function as information sources, public relations centers for the industry and, when necessary, as direct legislative lobbyists. They have, in short, made use of every opportunity and every device available to stave off federal regulation. Some of the prominent organizations in air pollution lobbying include Automobile Manufacturer's Association, Air Transport Association, Manufacturing Chemists Association, National Coal Policy Conference, National Coal Association, the American Petroleum Institute, and various railroads and barge lines involved in the transportation of coal for power generation.

The history of federal air pollution activity is even shorter than that of water pollution activity, and the first federal programs were not begun until a number of local air pollution control agencies had been established. The Air Pollution Control Act of 1955, the first federal effort, established a purely research operation in the Public Health Service. The Clean Air Act of 1963 amended this policy by expanding research activities and allowing for federal involvement in cases of interstate pollution. Similar to water pollution policy, the states could request federal intervention and ultimately federal legal action against pollution coming across state lines.

In 1963 the Public Health Service had been ordered to develop automotive emission standards as soon as possible, but these standards did not exist by 1965. In that year the Clean Air Act was amended to implement nationwide the emission standards developed in California. The federal standard, beginning in 1968, was to be enforced by HEW.

Current federal air pollution policy rests on the Air Quality Act of 1967. This act roughly provides for the following sequence of events:

1. The National Air Pollution Control Administration (NAPCA) designates "regional airsheds," generally surrounding large population centers. These airsheds or "air quality regions" may be interstate in character.

2. NAPCA prepares "air quality criteria" that describe the health effects of various individual pollutants and combinations of pollutants at various concentrations.

3. The local agencies for each airshed adopt "ambient air standards" consistent with and drawing on the NAPCA criteria.

4. The local agencies for each airshed develop implementation plans, including federal assistance of various kinds.

Even from this brief summary of federal air pollution policy it should be obvious that the great debates about state versus federal responsibility for this kind of regulation have for the moment been resolved in favor of the states. Federal policy is largely an exercise in "stimulative federalism" which depends for its ultimate effect on the resources committed to pollution fighting in each individual state. But in most states the expertise simply does not exist in sufficient depth to provide an effective counter to industry experts. Also, of course, the funding of local enforcement efforts must be approved by local legislative bodies, and it is unlikely that they will be less susceptible to lobbying activity than the U.S. Congress has been in the past.

The 1967 Air Quality Act is open to criticism on several grounds, and it is important to note that each weak point of the law fits into the kind of strategy industry representatives have used ever since pollution control efforts began. For instance, the law does not establish national emission standards. In its reliance on locally generated standards it opens the enforcement process to a variety of perennial complaints. In the first place, the local agency has to be able to monitor general air quality, since this is what the standards measure. But of course it is always possible to quarrel with the representativeness of a sampling procedure, and really reliable sampling is probably beyond the financial capabilities of most local agencies. Common industry arguments in the past have taken just this direction.

Sampling the emissions of given factories, as would be required for regulation based on emission standards, is also expensive and unreliable, of course, but at least then the burden of proof (and probably much of the expense) would be on the industry rather than on the public agency as it is now. Under current policy industries can say, in effect, that they have a kind of right to pollute unless they can be shown to be causing serious harm. When the local regulatory agency discovers that air quality standards are being violated, who can it prosecute? Industries, even those that are obviously polluting, can legitimately claim that they are being picked on without any specific evidence proving them guilty. This argument has often been raised in counterattacking lawsuits brought by industries, and even when the case has been without merit it has at least served to delay final regulatory action.

The lack of uniform national standards also contributes to another industry strategy, that of the implied or actual threat of reprisal for regulatory action. If one state sets standards higher than another's it must run the risk of losing the regulated industry to states with lower standards. Even in the absence of direct industry threats of this kind, local regulatory agencies often decide to pull their punches because of the possible adverse economic effects of zealous application of pollution standards, and the presence of such threats often simply confirms the fears of local agencies. This industry strategy has been very effective in the past because it forces local regulators and local politicians to consider possible adverse effects of regulation that are of genuine concern to them and their constituents. Under this kind of pressure a governor might decide that regulation is simply not worth the economic loss to his state, and he may pass the word down to the state's pollution control agency to go easy on enforcement.

An important part of the federal responsibility under the Air Quality Act also contributes to industry delaying tactics—the air quality criteria. The act commits NAPCA to a very large research task of a public health sort, discovering what amounts of the many pollutants in the air cause what kinds of health problems, and from these findings making recommendations for air quality standards. Industries can gain time here simply by questioning the evidence offered by NAPCA and calling for more research. The cigarette industry's attack on the Surgeon General's research into possible links between cigarette smoking and cancer is an exactly parallel example.

In fact, NAPCA has been pushing back its target dates for criteria reports on a number of major pollutants, and those cases where standards recommendations have been made have been criticized by industry spokesmen as arbitrary, premature, and based on inadequate evidence. Here again specific industries may be able to claim that they are being singled out undeservedly, and they may seek delays through judicial channels or through intercession by sympathetic hometown congressmen.

Industry spokesmen always seem willing to have more research done on a question of regulation, and they generally ask for more research before any regulatory action takes place. The energy industry has gone so far as to seek federal funding of antipollution research many times its own contribution in that area. Beginning in 1966, for example, the coal industry has contributed $107,000 annually to a joint research project with the power industry. At the same time the coal industry sought $100 million in federal research aid, and succeeded in getting $15 million.

To date NAPCA has obliged industry by shifting its effort increasingly to research and away from enforcement, devoting between 40 and 60 percent of its budget to research during the past several years. The NAPCA-industry consensus on the importance of government research, while indicating an apparently progressive industry attitude, actually puts NAPCA on the defensive. Industry spokesmen can say, in effect, "if NAPCA can't come up with anything, you certainly can't expect us to."

THE PROSPECTS FOR CHANGE

Pollution control, like other kinds of governmental regulation, depends for success on continued support for strong action from Congress and from the federal executive. In turn, continued public concern about pollution is a necessary energizer for these institutions. Without continuing pressure all along the line, it is likely that the implementation of pollution policy will again fall under the influence of the only actors always alert to pollution control—the major polluters themselves.

Actions in the 1970 lame-duck session of Congress show what can be done under public pressure. Over strenuous industry objections a law was passed requiring manufacturers to cut automobile pollution 90 percent by 1975 or face shutdown of their plants. Whether this law can legally be enforced or whether it will be enforceable politically remains to be seen, but at least it is on the books.

The same 1970 law opened the way for antipollution suits brought by individuals against corporate polluters. This addition to the antipollution arsenal may prove to be substantial because in effect it bypasses several steps in the regulatory process and substitutes citizen activists for bureaucratic administrators. Citizen groups presumably will not defer to industry wishes nor will they be timid in pressing cases that are less than perfect. On the other hand, the shift of attention to citizen activism throws pollution policy back to the kind of common law-neighborhood effects approach that has in theory always been available. The burden of proof will again be on the citizen plaintiff and each case will stand on its own merits. Thus pollution in Wisconsin will demand a Wisconsin lawsuit; policies in Arizona or New York will have little bearing elsewhere. The return to individual citizen initiative also means a return, at least in part, to contests between adversaries highly unequal in resources and legal skills. Friendly judges may be needed if citizen groups expect to get very far using this device.

It is obvious, even with the advances of the last few years, that the United States is still a long way from having an effective environmental protection policy. Achieving such a policy requires a positive approach emphasizing environmental quality, nationwide emission standards and effluent standards, and massive and continuing regulatory effort backing up those standards. The last of these steps remains the most difficult, and it may be necessary to discover new sources of political support for regulation before much more stringent control is possible.

Recent administrative action by the Food and Drug Administration points to one such source. In confiscating foodstuffs suspected of mercury contamination, the FDA has driven a wedge between food processors and industrial mercury users, groups that would otherwise take similar positions on pollution matters. If pollution becomes so serious that it spills over into other regulatory areas, the hand of pollution control agencies may be greatly strengthened. In the interim, pollution control must continue to limp along with the fickle and uncertain support of American public opinion.

Pollution control politics and, indeed, the politics of welfare reform and wage and price controls all share these common features: each is a mixture of special interest pleas and representations from broader, "public" interests. When the public is quiescent and its would-be spokesmen preoccupied elsewhere, special interests will naturally dominate the policy process. Special interest politics in these areas, as in many others that this book might have considered, is generally status quo politics to which the analysis of public problems is largely irrelevant. If issue analysis of the sort practiced in this book is to be useful, the customary patterns of economic policy making must be widened to encompass plausible alternatives to current policy. But how that expansion might occur is, aside from the few remarks here, a subject beyond the scope of this book.

Notes

[1] Estimates for 1970 by National Air Pollution Control Administration.

[2] Cited in John C. Esposito, ed., *Vanishing Air* (New York: Grossman, 1970), pp. 88–89.

[3] National Air Pollution Control Administration, *National Emission Standards Study*, March 1970.

[4] Based on data in *Congressional Quarterly Weekly Report,* April 24, 1970, p. 1138.

[5] Joint Committee on Atomic Energy, "Environmental Effects of Producing Electric Power," 1969, p. 1.

[6] "Environmental Effects," p. 6.

[7] "Environmental Effects," p. 129.

[8] Figures cited in Esposito, *Vanishing Air,* p. 100.

Suggested Reading

Ideas, Ideologies, and Economic Development

An excellent survey of economic thought since the seventeenth century can be found in Daniel R. Fusfeld, *The Age of the Economist* (Glenview, Ill.: Scott, Foresman and Company, 1966). The early philosophy of mercantilism is covered by Arthur E. Monroe, *Early Economic Thought* (Cambridge, Mass.: Harvard University Press, 1945). Harry W. Laidler, *Social-Economic Movements* (New York: Thomas Y. Crowell Co., 1948), and Philip Taft, *Movements for Economic Reform* (New York: Rinehart and Company, 1950) provides valuable background on the origin of socialist ideologies.

The unique pattern of American economic thought and economic development is, of course, the subject of very substantial historical scholarship. Louis M. Hacker, *The Triumph of American Capitalism* (New York: McGraw-Hill Book Company, 1965) is a useful description of the interplay of political and economic forces in American economic development up to the twentieth century. Thomas C. Cochran, *The American Business System* (Cambridge, Mass: Harvard University Press, 1957) extends this approach through the 1950s. Two major nineteenth-century social philosophies are examined in Richard Hofstadter, *Social Darwinism in American Thought* (Boston: Beacon Press, 1955), and Sidney Fine, *Laissez Faire and the General-Welfare State* (Ann Arbor: University of Michigan Press, 1964). F. X. Sutton *et al., The*

American Business Creed (Cambridge, Mass.: Harvard University Press, 1956); James W. Kuhn and Ivar Berg, *Values in a Business Society* (New York: Harcourt, Brace & World, 1968); and John H. Bunzel, *The American Small Businessman* (New York: Alfred A. Knopf, 1962) analyze contemporary business philosophies.

A number of books concentrate on concrete policy rather than ideology. Pragmatism in local economic development policy is described in three important books; Louis Hartz, *Economic Policy and Democratic Thought: Pennsylvania 1776–1860* (Cambridge, Mass.: Harvard University Press, 1948); Milton Sydney Heath, *Constructive Liberalism: The Role of the State in Economic Development in Georgia to 1860* (Cambridge, Mass.: Harvard University Press, 1954); and James Neal Primm, *Economic Policy in the Development of a Western State: Missouri, 1820–1860* (Cambridge, Mass.: Harvard University Press, 1954). Carter Goodrich, ed., *The Government and the Economy: 1783–1861* (Indianapolis: The Bobbs-Merrill Company, 1967) presents a collection of contemporary documents from both the national and state levels.

The Modern Economy and Economic Policy Making

There is no shortage of materials on that ubiquitous feature of the modern economy, the corporation. Two early books on the corporation are Adolf A. Berle and Gardiner C. Means, *The Modern Corporation and Private Property* (New York: The Macmillan Company, 1937), and Thurman Arnold, *The Folklore of Capitalism* (New Haven, Conn.: Yale University Press, 1937). These works have been updated in Adolf A. Berle, *The Twentieth Century Capitalist Revolution* (New York: Harcourt, Brace & World, 1954) and Gardiner C. Means, *The Corporate Revolution in America* (Cambridge, Mass.: Harvard University Press, 1960). Recent criticisms of the social consequences of corporate growth also include Michael D. Reagan, *The Managed Economy* (New York: Oxford University Press, 1963), and John Kenneth Galbraith, *The New Industrial State* (Boston: Houghton Mifflin,

1967). Two useful collections of articles are Edward S. Mason, ed., *The Corporation in Modern Society* (New York: Atheneum, 1967), and Andrew Hacker, ed., *The Corporation Take-over* (New York: Harper & Row, 1964). The blurring of the governmental-nongovernmental distinction in many areas of public policy is criticized in Henry S. Kariel, *The Decline of American Pluralism* (Stanford, Calif.: Stanford University Press, 1961); Granc McConnell, *Private Power and American Democracy* (New York: Alfred A. Knopf, 1967); and Theodore J. Lowi, *The End of Liberalism* (New York: W. W. Norton and Company, 1969).

The sprawling machinery of bureaucratic regulation has only been sampled by political scientists. Samuel Krislov and Lloyd D. Musolf, eds., *The Politics of Regulation* (Boston: Houghton Mifflin, 1964) is a comprehensive reader, while Marver H. Bernstein, *Regulating Business by Independent Commission* (Princeton, N.J.: Princeton University Press, 1955) and Louis M. Kohlmeier, Jr., *The Regulators* (New York: Harper & Row, 1969) provide more general and theoretical treatments. Texts such as Emmette S. Redford, *American Government and the Economy* (New York: The Macmillan Company, 1965) survey policy problems in a variety of regulatory areas. Two examples of specific area studies are Charles F. Phillips, Jr., *The Economics of Regulation: Theory and Practice in the Transportation and Public Utility Industries* (Homewood, Ill.: Richard D. Irwin, 1965), and Herbert R. Northrup and Gordon F. Bloom, *Government and Labor* (Homewood, Ill.: Richard D. Irwin, 1963).

Macroeconomic policy in the past decade has given rise to an extensive literature of the "current history" variety. Among the books written by "insiders" are Walter W. Heller, *New Dimensions of Political Economy* (New York: W. W. Norton and Company, 1967); Arthur M. Okun, *The Political Economy of Prosperity* (Washington, D.C.: The Brookings Institution, 1970); Charles L. Schultze, *The Politics and Economics of Public Spending* (Washington, D.C.: The Brookings Institution, 1968); Herbert Stein, *The Fiscal Revolution in America* (Chicago: University of Chicago Press, 1969); and James L. Sundquist, *Politics and Policy:*

The Eisenhower, Kennedy and Johnson Years (Washington, D.C.: The Brookings Institution, 1968). Valuable supplementary sources include E. Ray Canterbery, *Economics on a New Frontier* (Belmont, Calif.: Wadsworth Publishing Company, 1968); Jim F. Heath, *John F. Kennedy and the Business Community* (Chicago: University of Chicago Press, 1969); and Hobart Rowen, *The Free Enterprisers: Kennedy, Johnson and the Business Establishment* (New York: G. P. Putnam's Sons, 1964). The official presidential viewpoint is readily available in the annual *Economic Report of the President* and the *Annual Report of the Council of Economic Advisers.*

The Federal Reserve Board is more reticent about the specifics of its own activities, but its periodic publication *The Federal Reserve System* gives the general flavor of the Board's policy role. Other sources on the Federal Reserve Board include George L. Bach, *Federal Reserve Policy Making* (New York: Alfred A. Knopf, 1950), and Neil H. Jacoby, *United States Monetary Policy,* rev. ed. (New York: Frederick A. Praeger, 1964).

The congressional side of the economic policy process is treated in Richard F. Fenno, Jr., *The Power of the Purse* (Boston: Little, Brown, and Company, 1966); John F. Manley, *The Politics of Finance* (Boston: Little, Brown, and Company, 1970); and Aaron Wildavsky, *The Politics of the Budgetary Process* (Boston: Little, Brown, and Company, 1964). Lawrence C. Pierce, *The Politics of Fiscal Policy Formation* (Pacific Palisades, Calif.: Goodyear Publishing Company, 1971), attempts to synthesize the congressional and executive approaches to fiscal policy. Robert S. Benson and Harold Wolman, eds., *Counterbudget* (New York: Praeger Publishers, 1971), a book sponsored by the National Urban Coalition, argues that spending priorities could be radically altered within the normal incremental budgetary process.

Inflation, Wage, and Price Controls

Nearly all the writings on the subject of inflation and proposals for the solution of this problem take a purely economic point of view.

In addition, much of the literature dates to the Korean war and World War II control experiences, and may seem antiquated in the 1970s. A sample of this early work includes John Kenneth Galbraith, *A Theory of Price Control* (Cambridge, Mass.: Harvard University Press, 1952); Seymour Harris, *Price and Related Controls in the United States* (New York: McGraw-Hill Book Company, 1945); Abba P. Lerner, *The Economics of Controls* (New York: The Macmillan Company, 1957). Two early books considering some of the political aspects of controls are E. G. Nourse, *Price Making in a Democracy* (Washington, D.C.: The Brookings Institution, 1944), and Emmette Redford, *Administration of National Economic Control* (New York: The Macmillan Company, 1952). The activities of the Office of Price Administration are reported in Harvey C. Mansfield and associates, *A Short History of OPA* (Washington, D.C.: Office of Temporary Controls, Office of Price Administration, 1948).

Two publications by the Committee for Economic Development, *Defense Against Inflation* (New York: Committee for Economic Development, 1958) and *Further Weapons Against Inflation* (New York: Committee for Economic Development, 1970) provide a brief introduction to the problem of inflation in peacetime. By far the most comprehensive source is the multi-volume Joint Economic Committee, *Staff Report on Employment, Growth and Price Levels,* 86th Cong., 1st sess. (Washington, D.C.: U.S. Government Printing Office, 1959).

Several of the "insider" books from the Kennedy and Johnson years are valuable sources on the wage and price guidelines of the 1960s, especially Walter W. Heller, *New Dimensions of Political Economy* (New York: W. W. Norton and Company, 1967), and Arthur M. Okun, *The Political Economy of Prosperity* (Washington, D.C.: The Brookings Institution, 1970). John Sheahan, *The Wage-Price Guideposts* (Washington, D.C.: The Brookings Institution, 1967), and George P. Shultz and Robert Z. Aliber, eds., *Guidelines, Informal Controls, and the Market Place: Policy Choices in a Full Employment Economy* (Chicago: University of Chicago Press, 1966), provide additional points of view. E. Ray Canterbery, *Economics on a New Frontier* (Belmont, Calif.: Wadsworth Publishing Company, 1968), and Grant McConnell, *Steel and the Presidency, 1962* (New York: W. W. Norton and Company, 1963), treat the guidelines as instances of Presidential persuasion. Arthur F. Burns and Paul A. Samuelson debate competing solutions in Burns and Samuelson, *Full Employment, Guideposts and Economic Stability* (Washington, D.C.: American Enterprise Institute for Public Policy Research, 1967).

Poverty and Welfare Reform

Writings on the poverty question fall into three broad categories: books describing the problem, pieces criticizing current programs, and works proposing new programmatic solutions.

The early 1960s saw a steady flow of descriptive efforts, beginning with Michael Harrington, *The Other America* (New York: The Macmillan Company, 1962). Other books of this type are Margaret S. Gordon, ed., *Poverty in America* (San Francisco: Chandler, 1965); Oscar Ornati, *Poverty Amid Affluence* (New York: Twentieth Century Fund, 1966); and Leo Fishman, ed., *Poverty Amid Affluence* (New Haven, Conn.: Yale University Press, 1966). The Current Population Reports series of the United States Bureau of the Census is an invaluable source of basic poverty statistics.

Robert Theobald, *Free Men and Free Markets* (Garden City, N.Y.: Doubleday Anchor, 1965), and National Commission on Technology, Automation and Economic Progress, *Technology and the American Economy* (Washington, D.C.: U.S. Government Printing Office, 1966), examine automation and its impact on income distribution from competing viewpoints. David Bazelon, *The Paper Economy* (New York: Vintage Books, 1965), and Richard H. Tawney, *Equality* (New York: Capricorn Books, 1961) argue for income equality as a necessary condition for personal freedom.

Existing welfare programs are reviewed and critiqued in Winifred Bell, *Aid to Dependent Children* (New York: Columbia University Press, 1965); Joseph A. Kershaw, *Government Against Poverty* (Washington, D.C.: The Brookings Institution, 1970);

Sar A. Levitan, *Federal Aid to Depressed Areas* (Baltimore: Johns Hopkins University Press, 1964); Sar A. Levitan, *The Great Society's Poor Law: A New Approach to Poverty* (Baltimore: Johns Hopkins University Press, 1969); Peter Marris and Martin Rein, *Dilemmas of Social Reform* (New York: Atherton Press, 1967); Daniel P. Moynihan, *Maximum Feasible Misunderstanding* (New York: Free Press, 1969); United States Senate, Subcommittee on Employment, Manpower, and Poverty of the Committee on Labor and Public Welfare, *Examination of the War on Poverty,* 90th Cong., 1st sess. (Washington, D.C.: U.S. Government Printing Office, 1967); and Gilbert Y. Steiner, *Social Insecurity: The Politics of Welfare* (Chicago: Rand McNally & Company, 1966).

Theodore R. Marmor, ed., *Poverty Policy* (Chicago: Aldine-Atherton, 1971), offers a compendium of approaches to the solution of the poverty problem. Also useful as an overview is United States Congress, Subcommittee on Fiscal Policy of the Joint Economic Committee, *Income Maintenance Programs,* 90th Cong., 2nd sess. (Washington, D.C.: U.S. Government Printing Office, 1968). Specific techniques are presented in Eveline M. Burns, ed., *Children's Allowances and the Economic Welfare of Children* (New York: Citizens' Committee for Children of New York, 1968); Christopher Green, *Negative Taxes and the Poverty Problem* (Washington, D.C.: The Brookings Institution, 1967); Alfred J. Kahn, *Studies in Social Policy and Planning* (New York: Russell Sage Foundation, 1969); and Joseph A. Pechman, Henry J. Aaron and Michael K. Taussig, *Social Security: Perspectives for Reform* (Washington, D.C.: The Brookings Institution, 1968).

Air and Water Pollution

Environment, ecology, and pollution—the catch words have become almost interchangeable—refer to a large and vaguely defined policy area. The underlying intellectual basis of pollution concern, the science of ecology, is lucidly introduced in Barry Commoner, *The Closing Circle* (New York: Alfred A. Knopf, 1971).

Among the solution-oriented approaches, two extremes stand out: emotionally charged muckraking and relatively detached economic analysis. In the first class, Dr. Paul R. Ehrlich and Richard L. Harriman, *How to Be a Survivor* (New York: Friends of the Earth Flash Ballantine Books, 1971); Frank Graham, Jr., *Disaster by Default* (New York: Curtis Books, 1966); and Robert Rienow and Leona Train Rienow, *Moment in the Sun* (New York: Ballantine Books, 1967) are worthwhile reading. Publications of the various conservation and ecological groups such as the Sierra Club and the National Wildlife Federation also take a crusading tone. George R. Steward, *Not So Rich as You Think* (Boston: Houghton Mifflin, 1968) offers a less emotional view of natural resource depletion in the United States.

Economic approaches are represented by J. H. Dales, *Pollution, Property and Prices* (Toronto: University of Toronto Press, 1968); Edwin G. Dolan, *There Ain't No Such Thing as a Free Lunch* (New York: Holt, Rinehart and Winston, 1971); Neil Fabricant and Robert M. Hallman, *Toward a Rational Power Policy* (New York: George Braziller, 1971); and Resources for the Future, *Water Pollution, Economic Aspects and Resource Needs* (Washington, D.C.: Resources for the Future, 1962). A. V. Kneese and B. T. Bower, *Managing Water Quality: Economics, Technology, Institutions* (Baltimore: Johns Hopkins University Press, 1968) is a comprehensive treatment of its subject using traditional techniques; and Edward J. Cleary, *The ORSANCO Story—Water Quality Management in the Ohio Valley under an Interstate Compact* (Baltimore: Johns Hopkins University Press, 1967), describes one of the few success stories in water management.

Pollution politics, surprisingly, has received relatively little attention. J. Clarence Davies, III, *The Politics of Pollution* (New York: Pegasus Books, 1970), does deal with this subject, and the Nader study group report, John C. Esposito, ed., *Vanishing Air* (New York: Grossman Publishers, 1970) examines the operation of pollution control agencies and Congress from a muckraking viewpoint. Richard Neuhaus, *In Defense of People: Ecology and the Seduction of Radicalism* (New York: The Macmillan Company, 1971), while sharply critical of much of the ecology movement, does raise the hidden political question of who will pay for pollution control. Taking a more scholarly approach, Matthew A. Crenson, *The Un-politics of Air Pollution* (Baltimore: Johns Hopkins University Press, 1971), looks at the failure of air pollution agencies in large U.S. cities as a political problem rather than a technical one.

Index